I
DARKNESS
TO
LIGHT

The Redemption of a Soul
Bound by Addiction and Sin

Terry Bou

Terry Boucher
701-781-2021

APOSTOLIC PUBLISHING
HOUSE

Apostolic Publishing House LLC
Lumberton, MS 39455
www.apostolicpublishinghouse.org

From Darkness to Light / Terry Boucher. -- 1st ed.
ISBN 978-0-9976313-7-1

Edited by: McKenzi Sletten

Cover Design: Sonja Baker

IN DEDICATION TO MY MOM

I am immensely grateful for you, the amazing mom you have always been. You've never stopped loving me, even when I made life incredibly difficult for you. Thank you for all the sacrifices you've made for me, the many years of prayers and tears shed for me, and for instilling the Word of God into my life.

My mom and I.
Mother's Day
May 13, 2018
Lifepoint Sanctuary
Moorhead, Minesota

"Train up a child in the way he should go: and when he is old, he will not depart from it."
—PROVERBS 22:6

Even though I walked away from God, I knew where to come when I could not take any more of this world, and it's because of the way you raised me. I couldn't have asked for a better mom, and I know I would not be where I am today if it wasn't for you. I'll love you always.

FOREWORD

Terry's depiction of his life as a drug addict will bring you through many emotions. It will force you to see the grip that Satan has on our youth. Yet, throughout Terry's life, you will also see the miraculous hand of God and be encouraged to never give up or stop praying for those who are caught up in this lifestyle.

I was Terry's primary Sunday School teacher when he was in the third and fourth grade. Terry and his brother were full of life, a rambunctious pair. They were fun-loving and played off each other, taunting the other children as well as their teacher. However, I noticed that when Terry was alone, he was polite, attentive, and eager to learn. He even participated in Bible quizzing. However, as time went on, the influence of his friends would become evident in the decisions Terry would ultimately make.

I remember speaking with Terry's mom one morning after church. She asked about a program we were just starting called Life In Focus Ministry. The court judges would refer parolees to go through courses in substance abuse, anger management, parenting, and finances. She was very excited and hopeful that this was just what Terry needed. It still amazes me how God can provide what people need at the right moment in time with the right people. He really is an on-time God!

Terry was mandated by the judge to go through the Life In Focus Ministry courses. It was not easy. He had to work through raw emotions and negative thinking and, especially, learn to control his anger. The concepts were life-changing. However, like most changes, it took time to alter his way of thinking. There were times Terry struggled with drugs and the lifestyle that God was desperately trying to bring him out of. But, for the grace of God, and the help of those dedicated to see his recovery through, as well as his perseverance to get back up each time, Terry became an overcomer and is a living testimony of the transforming power of God!

As you read his book, you will see the mighty hand of God on Terry and the many miracles that literally saved his life numerous times. Through the grace of God, many prayers, and counseling, Terry is sober and living his life for Christ. Along with his experiences and the Gospel of Jesus Christ, Terry's goal is to reach those suffering from drug addictions and whose lives have no hope. I am very proud and thankful for the man he has become and his goal of furthering the kingdom of God. He is living life to the fullest for Jesus and enjoying every minute.

I would like to encourage every Sunday School teacher, Youth minister, pastor, and lay person that, whether you are preaching, teaching, or counseling, your fervent prayers and tears never go unanswered and are never in vain. The Word of God and the truth of the Word will always abound in the hearts of the ones you lift up in prayer.

I am grateful for our savior, Jesus Christ. I want to give Him praise for His unfailing love, mercy, and grace that has brought Terry and everyone who is willing to a place of repentance and redemption.

"...If God be for us, who can be against us?"

—ROMANS 8:31

- Sister Javana Wantuck Tutterrow

ACKNOWLEDGEMENTS

I owe an enormous debt of gratitude to all those who have not only been involved in the making of this book but to all those who have prayed for me and helped mold me into who I am today. This book would not have been possible without you and Jesus Christ. I pray you are all greatly blessed for your contributions.

First, I would like to give thanks to Michelle Pace. I had entertained the idea of writing a book about my testimony many times before. However, the last time you encouraged me to put my testimony down on paper, my inspiration grew to pursue this project. I would also like to thank you for putting me in contact with Sis. Baker at Apostolic Publishing House, for taking the time to offer me insight on my manuscript, as well as for your help with the introduction. Your words of encouragement gave me the push I needed to begin this project.

Additionally, I want to thank the Harpoles and their church for investing in me as a child. Thank you for remaining loving as I began to rebel and push back against the church, and thank you to the Sommer family for taking me in and giving me a place to stay when I first came to Fargo, ND and was trying to get my feet back on the ground and established.

My gratitude is also extended to my Aunt Sandy. Thank you for your love and prayers throughout the years of my downward spiral.

I thank Javana Wantuck Tutterow for writing the foreword of this book for me. All the prayers and time you invested in me as a young child in Christ are not forgotten.

Had my church family at Cornerstone Apostolic in Wentzville, MO not loved and accepted me with open arms, I would have not had a chance. Cornerstone Apostolic, you took me in and loved me unconditionally. Thank you for the countless hours you invested in me. You were the representation of what a true church should look like. Thank you to all my Life In Focus Education teachers who poured into me and inspired me to press forward, and to all the McCartys for loving me and showing me a true godly example.

To my best friend Barb and her husband Tony, I thank you for always being there for me, loving me unconditionally, coming to my place in the middle of the night to pray for me when no one else would, and for being a godly example to me. You always encouraged me to keep getting back up and keep moving forward. When I was in a new place and learning to cope with reality without substances, you were always there for me, and I would have given up long ago had you not been in my life.

I would like to thank Nikki Matzke for doing the initial edit when the book was in its most undeveloped state. Thank you for being my thesaurus and helping me pick my chapter titles.

I thank my pastor's wife, McKenzi Sletten, for taking so much time to do the final edit and for writing the description on the back cover. Thank you also for your help with the Gospel message portion of this book. You did an amazing job, and I am so thankful for your help with it all.

Thank you to my pastor, Andrew Sletten, who truly is a man of God and a man of mercy. You have so much love for people and such a good heart. Even when you are not personally teaching me something, I am always being taught by your actions and decisions. I am ever so grateful that God has placed you in my life.

To all of my brothers and sisters here at Antioch Church in Fargo, North Dakota, I couldn't be happier with where I am and with all the people within our church. I am thankful to have such a kind and loving family here to encourage me and to just be there in times of need. From when it was just a few of us in the basement till now, it has been great, and I am excited to see what the Lord unfolds for us in the future.

Sonja Baker, thank you for helping guide me through each step of the process in getting my book published. You have been so patient and wonderful to work with from the very first phone call. I would also like to acknowledge the rest of Apostolic Publishing House for putting my book together and for giving me the opportunity to share my testimony with a larger audience. I am very pleased with the end result and thankful you all embraced my vision for the book cover.

I would also like to thank Wave Photo by Aislinn Kate in Pensacola, FL, for doing such a great job with taking the cover photos for this book. The entire process was smooth from start to finish. Thank you for being friendly and professional, and for capturing exactly what I wanted in the photos.

A big thank you to Brother Nathaniel Urshan as well, for allowing me to use a quote from one of his podcasts in the Gospel message at the end of the book, as well as to all the men and women of God who have kept the faith and are persistent is preaching the word of God. You have made it possible for people like me and so many others to have the opportunity to experience this wonderful salvation. 1 Corinthians 1:21 says, "For after that in the wisdom of God the world by wisdom knew not God, it pleased God by the foolishness of preaching to save them that believe."

And last but certainly not least, I thank my Lord and Savior, Jesus Christ. Your mercies truly are new every day. Your love is never-ending. You saved me from a life in prison and a death before salvation. You have done all of this countless times. These are just the times I am aware of. Only You know how many situations You protected me from that I have no knowledge of. I cannot thank You enough for your love and mercy. I would be nothing without You. May You continue to guide and direct my paths and keep my faith from failing when I am tried in the fire.

- *Terry Boucher*

CONTENTS

CHAPTER ONE

INTRODUCTION

"In the beginning God created the heaven and the earth."
—GENESIS 1:1

When God created the heaven and the earth, He did so by merely speaking it all into existence. The dry land and seas, celestial bodies, plants, and animals were all created by God's spoken word. But when it came to the creation of man, scripture tells us that God formed him out of the dust of the ground and created him in the very image of God. Then He breathed the breath of life into man, and man became a living soul. God's desire in creating man in this way was to have a creation that would commune with Him and carry out the will of God on the earth.

Every person has a unique God-given purpose and story. Many times, after sharing my personal testimony of all God has done for me, I have been encouraged by others to write my story. I must admit that I, too, had these thoughts but would brush them off in the wind as quickly as they came. But not too long ago, God prompted me to write. This time it felt different, not just a thought soon to be forgotten. God imbedded it into my heart and mind. I knew that the season and time were right. I am not writing this by happenstance. It is my appointed time to declare the mercy and love God has shown me.

"To every thing there is a season and a time to every purpose under the Heaven."

—ECCLESIASTES 3:1

It is my desire that this detailed testimony of my life will give glory to God for all He has done and continues to do for me. May it serve as a tool to increase the faith of those who read it and spark anticipation for the miraculous things God will do in the future, for with God, nothing is impossible. May it serve as a reminder to myself and others of how amazing, loving, and merciful God is. No valley is so low that God cannot bring you out of it. Jesus stands at the door of our hearts and knocks, just waiting for us to answer.

"Behold, I stand at the door, and knock: if any man hear my voice, and open the door, I will come in to him, and will sup with him, and he with me."

—REVELATION 3:20

I am a walking miracle. I should have been dead countless times but for the Grace of God. God spared my life from car wrecks, violent fights, stabbings, and drug overdoses. My prayer is for this testimony to reach a hurting soul…that it would speak to the one who thinks they are too far gone to make their way back to God, to the one who has lost all hope and strength to keep fighting. I used to be that one, and I tell you it is not too late!

In Matthew 14, Peter attempts to walk on the water to Jesus. As he starts to notice the raging storm all around him, he begins to focus on the problem and not the Problem-Solver. He starts to lose his faith and begins to sink, but Jesus reaches down and pulls him up out of the water.

Look to Jesus, reach up for Him, and He will begin to pull you out of the sin that has overtaken your life.

*"He lifted me up from the pit of despair, out of the mud
and mire. He set my feet on solid ground and steadied me
as I walked along."*

—PSALM 40:2 (NLT)

"THE ROAD LESS TRAVELED"

On life's journey, you face difficult roads.
Encounter lots of rain, and carry heavy loads.

Things will happen, things will go wrong.
The drive may become bumpy, and seem very long.

You get a flat tire, you are running out of gas.
You start asking ME, how long will this trip last?

It has become dark, and no sign in miles.
Turn after sharp turn, traveling life's little trials.

Your eyes grow tired, and head starts to nod.
Wake up! Wake up!, For I am your God!

You have to keep driving, you have to fight.
It will not last forever, and soon will be light.

The sun will rise, and you will make it.
Just when you thought, you couldn't take it.

I am the way, the truth and the life.
Even on the darkest roads,
In the middle of the night.

CHAPTER TWO

SETTING SAIL

O n August 29, 1983, my life journey began in Joliet, Illinois. When I was only five months old, my dad passed away from leukemia, leaving my mom to take care of me and my slightly older brother by herself. We continued living in Illinois until I was three years old when we moved to Missouri, where most of my mom's family lived.

Despite not having a dad, my brother and I had a good life. My mom made the best of everything and always put us first. Every year, we would go on a fun excursion, like the ocean, Disney Land, Universal Studios, or some kind of theme park with rides. My brother and I loved riding rollercoasters. They were such an adrenaline rush for us. That stomach-dropping feeling we got as we plunged down the track at high speeds was the high point of our summer vacations.

We always went camping once a year at a nostalgic campground. Being there felt like the good old days before life was drowned out by all the busyness and chaos of the world. There was a pool, an arcade, and a little store with old-fashioned ice cream. We went on hay rides, rode on paddle boats, and caught fish in several stocked ponds on the campground. We were always doing something and going somewhere, and I couldn't complain in the least.

My mom raised my brother and me in church from the beginning. I remember hiding under the church pew with coats hanging down the back, pretending it was my little fort. We went to a Pentecostal church, which was very lively and full of God's Spirit. At the time, I did not understand why people ran around and shouted so much, but I did know to keep my little fingers inside the fort so they wouldn't get stepped on as people ran the aisles.

I enjoyed going to church and dressing up in my Sunday best each week. I even thought it was cool to wear a tie to church. As I grew older, I started to understand more and really enjoyed being in the presence of God. People were exuberant in their worship because they were excited about what the Lord had done in their lives. They were rejoicing as they felt God's presence. I have often heard people make jokes about how those in a Spirit-filled church jump up and down and holler. But it's really no different than the way people act over a sports game. In my opinion, many sports fanatics act crazier. They paint themselves and stand outside in the freezing cold with no shirts on. It saddens me that people are ridiculed for their enthusiasm for their Savior.

At an early age, I became involved in Bible Quizzing. I had a passion for memorizing scripture and loved the competition, especially buzzing in before the question was fully asked. Even though I was a little rambunctious, I was a pretty good kid. I was involved in church, always made straight A's in school, and won many trophies playing soccer and baseball. I also helped my mom out in the yard, raking leaves and pushing a lawn mower. She taught me the value of a good work ethic at a very early age, and for that, I am ever so grateful.

Life was good. At the time, I had no idea how much pain and heartache I would soon endure, nor how much sorrow I would put others through due to my very poor choices and sin. As I look back on my life, I understand why separating ourselves from certain people, places, and things is so important. When you start going down the wrong road, it often does not seem all that bad at first. That's because what we choose to do or partake in on that wrong path is not always sinful. However, one bad choice starts a chain reaction. Like a ripple effect in the water, one small decision affects another, which, in turn, affects another…until the impact of that one small decision has grown and spread into something we never imagined.

You can't always see it from the shore you're standing on. It happens little by little, each choice not seeming so bad, not causing much change in the way you have always lived your life. But you're drifting slowly away, almost imperceptibly at first, until suddenly, you're so far away that when you look back, you can't even see where you used to be. The shore you were once standing on is out of sight.

Paul writes in I Corinthians 6:12, *"All things are lawful unto me, but all things are not expedient: all things are lawful for me, but I will not be brought under the power of any."* This means that not all things are sinful, but neither are they all beneficial. If there is something in your life that is drawing you away from God or leaving you with little or no time to pray and seek God, then it would be wise to reevaluate the priorities in your life. What you are doing may not necessarily be wrong in itself, but if it replaces God or distracts you from the things of God, then it is not expedient.

When I reflect on my past, I can see the turning point where everything started getting off track. It started with friends. I began hanging out with people a few years older than me, people who were always up to no good. A scripture I have found incredibly accurate by experience is in Proverbs.

"He that walketh with wise men shall be wise: but a companion of fools shall be destroyed."
—PROVERBS 13:20

We are easily molded by the company we keep.

I was about the age of twelve when I smoked my first cigarette. One of the kids I hung out with would steal cigarettes from his parents. One day, as he was getting ready to climb up a tree in my yard, he left his cigarettes on the ground and said to me, "Don't touch these." I had never really thought about smoking, but for some reason, after he was high up in the tree, I grabbed one and lit it up...not understanding how much that one decision would impact my life. That day started just one of many horrible addictions that would soon take over and control my life for many years to come. I started to crave cigarettes and soon was no longer smoking them because I thought it was cool. I was addicted to nicotine.

The devil wants to steal, kill, and destroy (John 10:10). I understand now that he begins his attacks when we are young and vulnerable. He starts off small and gradual, working on one thing at a time, and before we realize what is happening, our life is already out of control. All the things my mom tried to keep me from were for much greater reasons than I could have ever imagined.

As time went on, I became less interested in church. I was still going, but only because I was made to go. I started listening to heavy metal music, sneaking out of the house, and terrorizing the neighborhood. It was like a covert mission to sneak out, cause chaos, vandalize property, and not get caught. What started out as normal teenage delinquency, like going out in the middle of the night and knocking on people's doors really loud, eventually escalated to slashing tires, spray-painting property, and chucking rocks through windows.

Our friend Mikey's mom was always doing crafts or spray-painting rocks. This gave us access to all the paint we could ever want, and we did not let it go to waste. We enjoyed expressing our newfound acts of anarchy on people's property, bridges, and especially a nearby tunnel that ran underneath a major highway. The tunnel was one of our main hangouts because it was very secluded and hidden just along the edge of the woods.

We became very crafty and confident in our little escapades. One night, we decided to break into someone's shed. Instead of just busting off all the locks, we took the time to take them all apart, rob the shed, and put them back together as if nothing had ever happened. We were cool as cucumbers, without a care in the world.

The shed contained lots of fun items for us kids, one of which was a golf bag full of clubs and balls. We were enticed to go out to the side of the highway and drive golf balls right at the oncoming traffic. Amazingly, we never hit anyone.

My brother, our friend Mikey, and I also found a big tin of matches, which we did not waste any time putting to use. We set a fire and then went to a different spot and lit another fire. Then the homeowner caught us. He held us at gunpoint until the police arrived. I found out later that our first fire spread all the way up the grass about forty feet and down the highway a quarter of a mile. No legal trouble ever came out of it. All we were given was a slap on the wrist.

I was fascinated with fire. A favorite activity of mine was to take old beer bottles, fill them with gasoline, and make Molotov cocktails. I would start in the middle of the tunnel with about three of my home-made bombs and start busting them as I ran, escaping the flames of fury. It is a miracle I never caught myself on fire.

It may surprise you to know that I was only about 12 ½ years old when I committed all this destruction. It was also around the time when I first smoked weed. My friend, Mikey, had taken his sister's bag of marijuana, and we smoked a joint. I never thought it was a big deal. After all, it was only weed. It wasn't like it was some hard drug. So the progression of sin and addiction continued as I took another step towards inevitable destruction.

As I exited grade school and entered middle school, my behavior became more destructive. On one particular occasion, my friends and I visited a construction site where new homes were being built. Despite the fact that it was broad daylight, we started kicking in all the newly installed drywall in the houses. We caused an incredible amount of damage, but we weren't finished with our "fun" yet.

Later that day, we broke into a neighbor's home. We didn't even plan to take anything; we did it just for the thrill. Hours later, the police showed up, and my friend John, who was old enough to go to jail, was arrested. I was taken to City Hall, where I was questioned but released.

In the end, I was only given 24 hours of community service, which wasn't a big deal to me. All three days of community service entailed washing and cleaning K-9 unit police cars. The officer left us alone in the garage by ourselves. After he was out of sight, we popped a heavy metal cassette tape into his car and jammed out until we ran his battery completely dead.

Through all of this, I became even more irritated about having to go to church. I tried my hardest to get out of going every Sunday. I went to Sunday school but would hide as long as I could after it was dismissed, so I wouldn't have to join my mom for the remaining time in the church service. The pastor's wife found me while I was hiding out one time. When she grabbed me by the arm to start dragging me into the church, I kicked her in the shin as hard as I could. I was growing colder and colder, and I wasn't even that old yet.

Our church held service on New Year's Eve each year. There would be a couple of services with food and fellowship in between. During one of these events, my brother and I snuck out while everyone was praying and went to the highway to throw rocks at diesel trucks. This was one of our favorite past times as kids. We never threw them at the windows. We just hid in the ditches and waited for the front end of the trucks to pass. As soon as they did, we had enough time to jump up with our rocks and pelt the sides of the trailers. After having our fun for some time, we snuck back into the church without anyone knowing we were ever gone.

I was roughly 15 when I first drank alcohol. It was insane how it all happened. We went to a wedding reception for my cousin, and they played a game to see who the designated person for each table would be to get drinks from the open bar. Each table had a special napkin that was passed around the table while music played. When the music stopped, whoever had the napkin would be the designated drink person.

The music stopped while I had the napkin. Since I was so young, one would think the others would have given it to someone else. However, no one seemed to care. I couldn't believe it! So I began to get people drinks from the bar. It didn't take long before I started getting my own. I would get what was supposed to be a Shirley Temple, only with vodka added, or I would get whiskey and coke.

The bartender never questioned me. My brother and I were very drunk when it was over. No one seemed to notice, though, probably because they were intoxicated as well. That night, a whole new world of fun was opened up, at least in my eyes.

I began having my older friends get alcohol for me. I started sneaking alcohol into my room and drinking at home, as did my brother. I remember trying to clean the microwave one night because he was cooking a pizza totally wasted. He flipped it upside-down halfway through because it said, "rotate pizza." My friends and I also started meeting at an old abandoned bridge to drink. One night, while leaving, we saw flares and signs announcing a sobriety checkpoint up ahead. However, we were so drunk that instead of trying to turn around, we just continued on and admired how vibrant the flares looked until we pulled right up into the checkpoint.

We were all packed into my brother's car, and John was driving. The car was so packed that two people were riding in the trunk. The stop started out routine until the officers heard giggling coming from the trunk. When the trunk was opened, there were our friends, just laughing and having a good old time.

After that, the officers removed us from the vehicle and took us to a substation, where we waited for our parents to pick us up. Because we were all underage, we were charged with Minor In Possession. None of us seemed to really care that we had been picked up, and we were still all having our laughs. The girls with us just giggled most of the time and even asked the officers more than once if they had a curling iron they could borrow to do their hair. It was an eventful night for all of us.

At that point, I had only drank alcohol and smoked weed. But one night, as my friends and I once again ventured out to get alcohol at someone's house, we found that he also had something else to offer us...crack cocaine. At the time, I didn't know much about it. The guy just handed me a soda can with some crack on it and said I could take a hit, so I took my first hit of crack cocaine without hesitation. It took my breath away. Instantly, my mouth was so dry that I literally couldn't breathe or get any words out, and I began to panic.

After struggling for some time, somebody handed me a drink, which cleared it up right away, and I began to enjoy the high it gave me. However, my first experience with crack cocaine did not make me seek out more. It wasn't until high school that I began to use it heavily.

I had another older friend, Jimmy, who would regularly shoot pool at a bar. He found an opening on the back side of the building that a person could crawl through from the outside and then drop down a hatch right into the bar. Jimmy began robbing the place habitually, just taking two or three cases at a time so it would not be noticeable. Then he would show up at my window in the middle of the night, and I would sneak out and get drunk with him.

Jimmy also introduced me to meth. I snorted it the first time I did it, and it sure did burn. Aside from the burn, though, I liked how it made me feel. However, I did not have much access to it, so I pretty much just drank and smoked marijuana until high school, which was where I was acquainted with new people and more windows of opportunity to find drugs.

My brother was on the left, me on the right. Pinewoods Park in Wentzville, Missouri. This is the nostalgic campground my mom always took us to.

This is at the Jesse James Museum. My brother was on the right, me on the left. Little bit ironic since we both ended up behind bars eventually.

"IN THE VALLEY"

In the beginning God created
The Heavens and the earth
He is the one who goes before you
And has known you before birth

He has a plan
With the perfect outcome
So in your prayers ask
For thy will to be done

I know you're hurting
And you are in pain
But he wants you to use
This for your benefit and gain

I know it's hard
And easier said than done
But he never promised
It would be easy or fun

The Lord redeemed His people
And brought them out of Egypt
This isn't a fairy tale
Or a Hollywood script

He will give you trials
And tests for you to do
But what is put before you
He will bring you through

No need to worry
Or even fret
Because in the presence of your enemies
Thou preparest a table to be set

Your cup will run over
You'll dwell in the House of the Lord
He will protect you with
His shield and mighty sword

All we can do is
Learn to dance in the rain
Ask God for strength
And to ease the pain

He may let you bend
Or let you shake
But He will never give you more
Than you are able to take

So count it all joy
And use it to grow
Even when things are tough
And the answers you do not know

Because you are a child of God
And that will never change
Keep your head held high
And think not this trial strange

Sometimes things are hard
And you don't know the reason
But don't ever forget
It is only for a season

CHAPTER THREE

SUBMITTING TO EVIL

It was my freshman year of high school when things started to really spiral out of control, and my drug addiction intensified. I stopped going to church altogether at this point. My mom tried her best to keep me going. She even bribed me with money to get me through the doors, but I was too defiant. I was disobedient and made life extremely difficult for her. I cannot even fathom all the stress and grief I put her through.

I began to immerse myself in the goth culture. I dressed in dark clothing, grew my hair out really long, and listened to very evil music. I was being led away by the enemy.

The historic school shooting of Columbine, Colorado, occurred during my freshman year. After the news broke, all the teachers seemed to be on edge, but the horror of what happened didn't really phase me. I never liked seeing people get bullied, so I felt like the people who were shot probably had it coming to them. I continued on with my day in my cold-hearted state as if nothing had ever happened.

Later that night, I was looking to score some weed, so I went to the local movie theater to see what I could find. It was a hangout spot for teenagers, so I had high hopes of finding some. I asked around for a bit and was soon making a deal. The place was packed with people everywhere, so we quickly exchanged money, and the drugs were discreetly mine. After that, I was on my way to go get high.

I did not have a chance to look at what I bought with all the people around and never even thought about it, but when I got home and opened the bag up, I realized it was oregano. Livid, I stewed over what had happened the whole weekend and decided that first thing Monday morning, I was going to find that dude in the hallway and give it to him.

When I found him at school Monday morning, he was chatting with a group of people that I called the preps. While he was still talking, I approached him and slammed him up against the locker, and started going off on him. Everyone in the hallway stopped what they were doing as if they were frozen in time. All eyes were fixated on us. I screamed at him and told him I wasn't playing. As my emotions raged, I told him he had until the next day to get my money back, or he was dead.

After that, I went to my first-period class. It wasn't long until an officer pulled me out of class and brought me to the school office. Other people reported what I had said, and on top of that, they made up lies that I had a gun at school. One rumor going around was that I was going to kill everyone. Due to the recent news about Columbine, they took any kind of threat extremely seriously.

I sat in the office with the cops for hours while they interrogated me. They went over a series of questions, asking where the gun was in different ways. I kept telling them I didn't have a gun, but they would just look at me for a while and then say something like, "So who did you give the gun to?" I became very worked-up and started raising my voice at them, saying, "Listen, I don't have a gun! I didn't put a gun anywhere, and I didn't give a gun to anyone! There is no gun!" Finally, after hours of harassment, I was allowed to leave with my brother and friends.

When I went home that day, I had a bad feeling about everything. I was growing some marijuana plants in my closet but decided I needed to dispose of them quickly. Fortunately, I did because later that same evening, a bunch of cops showed up at my place to search for guns. The whole situation was blown way out of proportion. I didn't actually mean I was going to kill him. I just said, "You're dead," as in I'm going to beat the living tar out of you. Again, however, because it was just shortly after Columbine, it made everything worse.

Soon after this incident, I was on the bus waiting to leave for a varsity track meet. Despite drinking, doing drugs, and smoking cigarettes, I became interested in track in my seventh and eighth-grade year of school. It turns out I was a natural, especially in pole vaulting. I broke both pole-vault records in middle school, broke the record for junior varsity, and had broken the varsity record at practice. I just needed to go to a varsity meet to officially break that record as well.

Right before we left for the meet, where I hoped to set another record in pole vaulting, I was pulled off the bus for a drug test. They wouldn't let me go until the test results returned, causing me to miss the meet.

On top of that, I was suspended from school the next day. Due to my outburst, half the school wasn't showing up. The rumors of me shooting up the school had spread, and parents were fearful and not letting their kids come to school. The school said I could not come back until a psychiatric evaluation was done, stating that I was not a threat to anyone. I found myself suddenly being treated like a psychopathic murderer.

When I look back on the situation and consider everything, I don't blame the school for what they did. I enjoyed writing poetry back then, just as I do now, but my poetry at that time was dark and filled with murderous rhymes. I took a creative writing class, and those are the kinds of pieces I turned into my teacher. Patricia, a classmate of mine, told me that I would either become a famous writer or a serial killer one day.

I was very agitated with being kicked off the track team and out of school. Those two blows fueled my increasing anger for the school system and society in general. They sparked a rebellion against authority in me that began to spread like wildfire. I no longer had any desire to do anything productive with my life. The damage was done by the time I was allowed back into the school. My heart had blackened like a piece of coal.

From that time, my life began to spiral into deeper darkness. One day, while watching the 1997 MTV Music Awards, I saw a performance by Marilyn Manson. I'd never really listened to his music before, but he captured my attention that day. His performance started with such anger and hostility. He was ripping pages out of the Bible and going off on authority and Christians, who he made out to think were so high and mighty. It was full of rage and evil, but I found myself completely drawn in by it. It made me feel as though all the feelings of bitterness and anger I had built up inside of me were justified, and I had a reason to be infuriated with everyone.

I recorded it and watched it over and over, totally mesmerized. From that experience, I understand why what a person watches is so important. It isn't just a video or a movie. It is a tool of the devil, and one scene is all it takes for him to exert his influence over your life. That one video opened me up to a strong pull and desire into satanism.

Not long after that, I engulfed myself in watching movies about witchcraft. One movie was called "The Craft." It was about these girls who practiced witchcraft. They wanted to receive power and invite the evil spirits inside of them. In one part, they sat around reciting words from a book. Each one would invoke a spirit. They would pray and give permission for that spirit to enter them. After watching, I was compelled to do the same. I wanted that power of evil inside of me also.

One night, I brought some candles and paint out to a clubhouse that I had built in my backyard as a kid. I painted a giant pentagram symbol on the floor and lit candles at each tip of the pentagram. Then I sat in the middle of it and began praying to the devil. I prayed to the spirits of the watchtowers of the north, south, east, and west. In each of these prayers, I would invoke the spirit and give them permission to enter into my body and use me for their will.

I did the same with Satan. It is something I could have never imagined myself doing when I first started traveling down the road of sin. I've learned that sin will take you farther than you ever wanted to go and keep you longer than you ever intended to stay. I didn't realize at the time what a horrible thing I had just done by praying to the devil and evil spirits and giving them permission to use me for their purposes.

After that night, I became overtaken by the idea of evil. I started playing with Ouija boards, practicing black magic, and toying with voodoo dolls. I would curse God and tempt Him to kill me if He was so powerful. I would carve upside-down crosses in my arms and chest with razor blades. Though I knew the Gospel, a detestation for God had grown up inside of me, perhaps from the little seeds of sin that I had allowed to be planted along the way. They had grown as I fed them over time, and I was becoming the epitome of evil.

Spiritually speaking, whichever plant we feed, whether good or evil, is the one that will grow and overcome the other. If we are doing things against God's Word, the evil will be fed and continue to grow. Likewise, by doing good and feeding ourselves with God's Word, we allow the good seed to grow in our lives.

"Be not overcome with evil, but overcome evil with good."

—ROMANS 12:21

"STEAL, KILL, AND DESTROY"

The devil is seeking
For whom he may devour
You must be vigilant
And keep watch every hour

He wants to get your kids
Get them while they're young
Keep them away from God
With his lying tongue

Get them distracted
By what the world is doing
Tell them it's not bad
Don't worry what you're viewing

Introduce them to sin
With their friends at school
And if they don't join in
Then they must not be cool

If it makes you happy
It can't be that wrong
Just a quick trip with sin
It won't last long

We'll be right back
Just one more time
Then he wraps them in chains
With that famous line

You must protect them
With your prayers and love
Be wise as serpents
And harmless as doves

Train them up in
The way they should go
So they know who to lean on
When they are feeling low

hosts Trojan Relays

TROY'S ELSBERRY RELAY RESULTS INCLUDED

Bob Conn

Troy's Terry Boucher, above, clears the bar in the pole vault event. Boucher broke the existing record with his 10'9" vault.

Pole vault pictures. The newsaper clipping is where I broke the Junior Varsity record.

CHAPTER FOUR

SLIPPING DEEPER

My sophomore year didn't improve. I started dating Samantha, who also explored alcohol and drug use. With a new relationship came new friends and new drug connections. This was when I gained access to crystal meth on a much more regular basis. Samantha and I became very fond of each other. Every chance we got, we would hang out and get high. Her brothers were friends with a gang member and some really good meth cooks, so it was very easy to get our hands on a lot of drugs.

As time went on, my addiction progressed rapidly, and my life unraveled. I was using meth almost daily and staying up for days at a time without any sleep. I became paranoid and was rarely in reality. One day while high, I watched my friend Doug walk into the living room and just disintegrate into nothing, like dust in the wind. I got up and began calling his name and looking for him. I was so high that I didn't even realize I was obviously hallucinating.

These are the kind of hallucinations I saw daily. Many times, I heard people whispering my name ever so faintly. Leaves rolling across the road turned into animals that were running around. Mailboxes looked like people. One time, two leafless trees were standing side-by-side and blowing in a thunderstorm. To me, they looked like skeletons in action. While most people would be terrified by these bizarre scenes, I relished them. I looked forward to the feeling that came upon me at nightfall after being sleep-deprived and on meth.

There was a time when I was convinced I saw someone walk into my bathroom from down the hall. I picked up a knife and began opening each door, checking the rooms to ensure I did not somehow miss them as I headed toward the bathroom. But when I finally reached the bathroom, nobody was there.

I saw what many people on meth see and what the drug world calls "shadow people." A shadow person looks like a silhouette of a human that's either off in the distance or walking right beside you. You're always able to see them out of the corner of your eye. At the time, I brushed them off as mere hallucinations, just a part of being high, but I now firmly believe that certain drugs open a person's mind up to seeing into the spiritual realm, a realm we aren't usually able to see. I had gotten used to seeing these things.

My mom didn't know exactly what I was involved with, but she knew it wasn't good. She would always get onto me, which I took for nagging, but I realize now it was out of fear and concern. After doing meth for days with no sleep, I came home, and she tried having a conversation with me. I quickly became very agitated and told her I didn't want to hear it, but she kept talking. I remember finally telling her, "Listen, I'm really high on meth, and I just can't do this. If you keep talking, I'm going to flip out."

With the next words she said, I did just that. I picked up a full gallon of water and threw it right through the kitchen window. Then I went on a rampage, breaking stuff. When my mom went to call the police, I ripped the phone out of the wall and took off on foot. I began running at first, attempting to gain some ground in hopes that I could get to a road in the state park before the cops were called. My girlfriend lived on the other side of the park, and I planned to hide out there.

I made it almost five miles into the park with no sign of any police. I followed the road line in the woods, but I decided to come up on solid ground to make the trip easier. Whenever I heard a car coming, I would stick my thumb out to hitchhike, but they all kept passing me by. At last, I thought I heard a car slow down and thought maybe my luck had changed for the better. As it came to a stop, I turned around. It was the police. The officers started screaming and cussing at me and told me to get in their car.

The whole way to the police station, the officer lectured me about how I treated my mom, and rightfully so. Once we arrived at the station, they put me in full shackle restraints and escorted me to juvenile. I was there for about a day until they transferred me to a mental health facility. After about a week of undergoing mental health evaluations, I was released to my mom. Unfortunately, none of that slowed me down. Though I was apologetic while locked up, I went right back to the same old lifestyle upon being released.

Soon after this incident, I was introduced to LSD for the first time. Samantha and I went to a party where we each took two hits of it. When it started to kick in, it felt a little overwhelming. I had to tell myself to calm down and just go with the flow. Once I relaxed, I thought it was the most amazing drug I had ever done, a complete opposite of reality. Everything looked like it was expanding in and out, including the walls and people. The normal popcorn ceiling looked like raindrops rolling down a window, the carpet like a coral reef swaying back and forth in the ocean current. The night sky looked like a never-ending meteor shower. It was absolutely breathtaking, and it lasted for almost 12 hours. I loved every bit of it, and once again, another drug was added to my out-of-control addictions.

The rest of my sophomore year in school was hazy and filled with lots of substances and delinquent decisions. There was a time when we needed money for drugs, so we made up some fake LSD to sell to one of our friends. He really wasn't a friend we cared about, just more of an acquaintance we used if there was something we could get out of him.

We had a car battery that was busted open. The battery acid was leaking down the side, so we made up some strips of paper that looked like LSD and dipped them into the battery acid. The idea originated from the drug's street name, "acid." We took our "acid" and sold it to our buddy, telling him it was just freshly made. Later on, he said it was some good stuff, but it burnt his tongue. We weren't sure what to think. He was the type of person that would probably just say he got high to look cool, but at the same time, we didn't know what the effects of battery acid would actually do to a person. Either way, we made ourselves some money to take care of getting high.

Nothing changed the following year. I didn't live far from St. Louis, so we went to raves from time to time. They were wild. It seemed like once you got in the door, anything went. The raves were all set up for psychedelic drugs. Huge speakers and screens blasted techno music, so you could feel the music moving through your body. People were walking around everywhere selling drugs. One of my friends actually worked the raves selling drugs. The first time I ever did ecstasy was at one of these raves, along with another extremely dangerous drug called ketamine, or Special K for slang.

Ketamine is a tranquilizer made for horses, and it's a hardcore downer. Back then, people were robbing veterinary clinics for the tranquilizer. Then they would mix it with liquid, spread it out, and dry it into a powder. It was very strong, and it only took a small amount to get you high. Take too much, and your world would be turned upside down. On the street, it's called going into a "K Hole." The drug has similar effects to PCP and has also been used by sexual predators to incapacitate their victims.

It's only by the hand of God that I am alive. I was always mixing numerous kinds of these hard drugs in the same night. At times, I could feel my heart pounding out of my chest, or my heart would beat really fast, then slow down to hardly nothing, and then the pattern would repeat itself irregularly.

Sometime that same year, Samantha, her brothers, Brad and Doug, and I decided to go on a float trip in the southern part of Missouri. We brought along cases of beer and some marijuana. By the time we showed up at the campground, we were already wasted, and we started our eleven-mile trip the next morning the same way. There was so much beer in each of our kayaks that we often had to get out and push them until we got to deeper water because the excessive weight was causing them to drag on the river bed below.

We had heard stories about the cops hiding in the trees along the water's edge, patrolling and waiting to bust people. As ignorant kids, we would curse the cops while smoking weed, drinking beer, and throwing our cans into the river. It was all fun and games. Little did we know, a water patrol officer was watching us and taking pictures.

As we turned a corner a couple miles into our trip, we saw an officer with full gear come into the water towards us. He grabbed our kayaks and pulled us to the shore, and then he let us know he had been watching us since the night we got there. When it was all said and done, he confiscated our weed and made us pour out every single beer we had. Then we all received tickets and a scheduled court date for possession of marijuana and littering.

I remember driving hours for each court appearance until I was finally put on probation and given a stiff fine. One stipulation of my probation was that I could not be absent from school, which would later play against me.

As I was nearing the start of my senior year, I was still living life in the fast lane. My girlfriend's brother, Doug, was big into dirt bikes and was always up to something as well. He decided to steal a dirt bike from someone but didn't have anywhere to hide it, so he asked me if I could keep it at my house until he figured out what to do with it. When he got it to my place, we took the entire bike apart into pieces. I was going to take it to the woods that night, but I changed my mind and figured I could do it the next day after school, which turned out to be a big mistake.

I went to school the next day, which was also the first day of my senior year. While sitting at a lunch table, later on, I was approached from behind by a couple of cops, who said they needed me to come with them to the office. I honestly couldn't think of what they wanted at first, but they began to question me about the stolen dirt bike. I played stupid until they told me they had searched my place and found the dirt bike in pieces. Then they took me down to the police station to formally interrogate me. I kept telling them I didn't know it was stolen and didn't have anything to do with stealing it. They finished up their questions and brought me back to the school, and that was the last I heard about it for a little while.

Despite my drug use and unstable lifestyle, I somehow maintained very good grades. School just came easily to me, and I didn't have to put in much effort to pass my classes. By the end of my junior year of high school, I had accumulated all the credits I needed to graduate. Because of this, I could fail every class my senior year and still graduate, so I chose to stop trying altogether. I didn't care if my GPA was horrible or about going to college, just as long as I graduated.

I felt like I didn't have anything to lose and continued full speed ahead in my addictions. My senior year was filled with drugs, alcohol, school suspensions, and lawbreaking. Every week, I went out to do something deplorable, from vandalizing people's property to robbing places. I even showed up on my principal's doorstep with my brother and another friend of ours in the middle of the night just to cuss him out before taking off into the darkness.

The morning after that incident, the principal called us into his office. He gave us an ultimatum. Either we take in-school suspension, or he was going to call the police. Normally, we would have told him to get lost. However, the previous night, we also went into a neighborhood and slashed someone's tires. Before we could make our escape in my brother's car, the guy came out and started punching through the window. He ripped the front license plate off and then jumped on the hood of the car. We floored it to throw him off the hood and took off. He called the cops, and we were eventually pulled over at a gas station. Then we were searched and taken to jail for questioning.

We all kept our mouths shut during the questioning and agreed that we didn't know anything about tires being slashed. All we knew was some crazy guy flipped out on us. This incident put us in a predicament while sitting in the principal's office the next day. We didn't want any more involvement with the police over something that happened the same night, because it would be obvious that we had been out that night causing mischief. We chose the in-school suspension.

Throughout my senior year, I was doing meth on a regular basis. I would be awake for consecutive days and suffer through school, longing for the bell to ring so I could just get out of there. One day, I was sitting in class having hot and cold flashes. I wore a jacket because I felt like I was freezing, but I was sweating at the same time. I decided I needed to get out of there, so I pretended to be sick and arranged for my brother to pick me up at the last hour of the day. Because I didn't want to sit in the school office, I decided to go to the side of the school and smoke a cigarette while I waited for him.

While hidden away in the corner of the school building, I saw a police car pull up and an officer go inside the school. Between being paranoid from the meth and not respecting cops anyway, I decided it was best to take off on foot. My brother saw me and picked me up on the side of the road, and we went home. As soon as we got home, we went across the street to the neighbor's house to do some more meth. About 15 minutes later, that same police officer pulled into my driveway and knocked on the door.

Back then, anyone could call the courthouse to see if they had a warrant for their arrest, and they would actually tell them. After the officer left, I called the courthouse. I was informed I had a warrant out for Receiving Stolen Property on that dirt bike. The bond was $20,000 cash only. My instincts told me to hide out, but I knew I couldn't. I was only allowed to miss so many school days due to my probation from the float trip incident, and I would be getting in more trouble if I skipped school. I decided to take a few days to get my affairs in order and then turn myself in to get it over with.

I didn't expect to be out of jail for quite some time because neither my mom nor I had that kind of money. Surprisingly, at my arraignment in court the next morning, my bond was reduced to $7,500, of which I only had to pay ten percent. This gave me more of a chance to get out of jail and get back to school. My mom called a bondsman and was able to get me out on bond for only $750.

Neither of us had experience with this, so we did not fully understand how a bondsman worked. Once I was out of booking and in the jail lobby, my mom realized that she would not get her $750 back. This was a huge blow to her because we didn't have very much. When she tried to get her money back and have me go back to jail, I almost took off and ran, but the bondsman explained that it was too late to change what had already been done.

I was able to keep attending school, but eventually, my probation for the float trip ended, and then I was back to skipping school all the time. I missed so much school that the principal said they wouldn't let me walk for graduation if I missed much more. I honestly couldn't have cared less, but I knew it was a big deal to my mom, so I tried my best to slide by and be able to attend graduation.

Our school had incentives for people with all their credits completed. Because I had done this by the end of my junior year, I could have invested the remainder of my time in high school at a trade school. Then having learned a trade, I could have received a job placement upon graduating. However, instead of seizing that opportunity, I continued throwing my life away.

Astonishingly, I graduated high school despite the way I was living. After many court dates, I finally chose to take a plea deal for the stolen dirt bike. I had so much disrespect for authority. Rather than showing up looking halfway respectable, I thought it would be amusing to dye my hair bright blue the night before court. I remember trying to hurry up and get to my dope dealer's house and back before the bleach foils in my hair started to burn.

The plea deal was for two years of probation on the Receiving Stolen Property charge. I was placed on supervised state probation this time, and nothing had changed. Little did I know how much of a setup probation was if you did not follow all the guidelines. Later in life, I would realize how accurate the saying in NA and AA is, "Nothing changes if nothing changes."

Me on LSD in my sophmore year of high school.

"ONE AND ONLY"

You are Lord of Lords
And King of Kings
With all authority and power
Over everything

You are one God
Not three
Spirit manifested in the flesh
So we can see

You are Alpha and Omega
The beginning and end
You are closer than a brother
And my dearest of friends

You made a way for us
And died on the cross
Ate with sinners
To save the lost

You rose again
And conquered the grave
You break the yoke of bondage
And free the enslaved

You are the mighty one
The morning star
You took the stripes
And wore the scars

You are the Prince of Life
The Great I Am
The word of God
The innocent slain Lamb

You are the author and finisher
Rock and cornerstone
Our comforter when in need
So we are never alone

The first, the last
The Holy one
The one who was
And is to come

CHAPTER FIVE

CRASH DUMMY

In 2002, I found myself finally out of school and enjoying every bit of my freedom. I had a friend named Dan who lived way out in the country, where the houses were miles in between. It was the perfect area to throw big parties. One night, we threw a huge party out there with drugs and plenty of beer kegs. There was also a massive sound system, the kind typically found at concert venues, which we were able to use. Some of my friends had their own band, so they used their connections to invite another band to perform at the party. The band they invited had opened for a previous Marilyn Manson concert we had attended.

There were hundreds of people at the party. It seemed to be a huge hit that would be talked about for years to come. At some point in the night, I was with my friend, Grady, when his girlfriend, Debbie, told us that some guy had been hitting on her. We were lit up and decided we could not tolerate any of that. After searching for a while, Debbie was finally able to point the guy out amongst all the people.

Although it was my friend's girlfriend, I was feeling unrestrained and wanted a piece of the action. Grady and I decided that we would "rock, paper, scissor" for who got to hit the guy. I won the first game, but Grady suggested that we do two out of three for the win. We played two more times, with me coming out the winner. At that, Grady reluctantly said, "Okay, you can hit him."

I walked over to this complete stranger and confronted him about hitting on Debbie. When he began to talk, I blasted him as hard as I could in the face. It looked like his feet had been swept out from underneath him, and he hit the ground hard. In a panic, he tried to get up and take off running, but he was half-dazed and ran right into a tree, knocking him to the ground once more. And that was that. We all just laughed about what had happened and continued with our evening as though it was no big deal.

On another one of these summer evenings, my girlfriend, brother, and I were partying as usual. The evening was turning dark, and my brother had run out of alcohol. He kept demanding that we take him to get more, but we didn't want to drive anywhere. We were all pretty intoxicated at that point.

He finally decided he would drive to town and get it himself. The only problem was that Samantha's car was blocking him in. We wouldn't move the car because we knew he shouldn't be driving, and he continued to harass us for a good hour about letting him out.

Eventually, he turned very aggressive towards us. He started making all kinds of derogatory remarks toward my girlfriend, and I was sick of it. Angry, I moved her car and told him to get out of there. By that time, he was enraged as well. He got into his car, backed out, and took off down the gravel road, flying like a maniac. I remember thinking, "If he doesn't slow down, he's going to hit something," but I was also relieved he was gone.

After he left, Samantha and I went over to my neighbor's house to hang out, but we were only there about ten minutes when another neighbor showed up. He started telling us he had just heard on a police scanner that there was a terrible wreck just a few miles up the road. I knew it was my brother. We ran back to my mom's house, told her what had happened, and got her to drive us down the road.

As we approached the scene, there were flashing lights everywhere. It didn't look promising at all. The road was blocked off for quite some distance, so we got out and began to walk. We kept looking for a car, but all we could see were emergency vehicles.

We finally saw the horrific scene when we pushed past all the responders. There was his little red car, submerged inside someone's house! My heart sank. The part of the car we could see was completely mangled, and the whole wall of the home was caved in. It didn't look like anyone could survive a scene like that. It seemed like certain death.

Soon, a helicopter was landing in the middle of the road. We saw emergency personnel carrying a body on a stretcher up from the embankment the home was sitting on. Everything happened so rapidly. They wouldn't let us close enough to see him. All I could catch a glimpse of before the helicopter took off again were his boots sticking out from under the cover. We could not get any other information from the medical responders except that he was airlifted to St. John's Mercy Hospital in Saint Louis. This hospital was the one where extreme trauma patients were sent.

We rushed back home so my mom could get some things before leaving for Saint Louis. While she was frantically gathering her things, I rolled up a couple of joints to take with me. It's demented that I would even be thinking of weed in a moment like that, but I needed something to calm my nerves.

My mom knew that I used drugs, but I think she had lost hope of me ever changing over time. I never even told my mom that Samantha and I were going to smoke on the way there. We just lit up and smoked the weed right in her car on the way. I think she was too stressed to even notice or care.

Upon arriving at the hospital, we were told he was critical. He did not have a seatbelt on when he crashed and had serious head trauma.

His brain was bleeding and swelling as the doctors tried to keep him stable. I thought that at any minute, the doctors would be coming out to tell us that he did not make it.

By the grace of God, they were finally able to get him stable, but he was put into a medically induced coma. At the time, the doctors thought he would be in a coma for an extended period of time. But after about three days, the swelling in his brain started to subside. So they gradually started waking him up.

When he was finally awake, he was so drugged up that he hallucinated for days. He would try talking me into sneaking him out the window from the third floor. He even convinced my mom that I had snuck him out to the parking lot to drink alcohol. He was out of his mind. But after about three weeks, he had recovered enough to be released.

The doctors wanted us to keep a close eye on him. They said he could have short-term memory loss, and he could possibly slip into some kind of post-trauma episode and fall out. Basically, they were saying he wasn't out of the woods yet.

It really is an incredible story of God's hand protecting his life. The team investigating the wreck said that he had careened off the road at 90-100 mph based on the tire tracks. I had later gone to the scene in the daylight to see where he went off the road. What I saw was amazing. Not only did he veer off extremely fast, but he flew down an embankment that was at least thirty feet below.

After that, he traveled through about a 150-yard span of trees. When I went down to retrace the tracks, I couldn't believe what I saw. I could literally see the tire tracks repeatedly change to two wheels on one side right before a tree and then switch to two wheels on the other side before another tree. Back and forth, side to side, missing every single tree. It was as if God had lifted the car side to side, allowing him to miss them all!

This must have also allowed him to lose speed before plowing into the house, though he still hit it hard enough to make the wall topple in. The car sat halfway through the house, and the foundation was completely destroyed, but he had lost enough momentum to save his life. The car was upside-down and backward when it smashed into the home, and my brother had flown out the back window headfirst and was lying halfway in the house.

We later found out that the area of the house he smashed into was the homeowner's bedroom. However, he just happened to have fallen asleep on the living room couch that night, sparing his life. The whole scene was absolutely horrendous. There's no other explanation of all that transpired except that God's protective hand was in it.

My brother grew better day by day. One would think that an experience like that would shake a person so badly that they'd never drink again, but it didn't. A week or so after he was released from the hospital, we were all back at my neighbor's house drinking together again. It seemed that none of us had learned anything from it.

While my brother was still in the hospital, Samantha and I started smoking crack here and there. It didn't take long before we were hooked. Jared, our dealer, would rock up a half-ounce of coke a day into crack, so it was there whenever we wanted it. Even when we were trying to abstain from it for a while, Jared would call us up and ask if we wanted to get high. It was very addicting, and we couldn't say no. He knew that all he had to do was give us a few hits, and we would spend several hundred dollars before the night was over.

I had been working at a pizza place for a few years, and my addiction had gotten to the point where I began requesting pay advances from my job to buy crack. But one night, they wouldn't give me one because I hadn't worked enough hours to cover the advanced pay. I flipped out right in the middle of the restaurant. Families were eating in the dining room while I went on a rampage, cussing everyone out and smashing their open and closed sign to pieces. I left fuming with anger and never returned to work, assuming I was fired.

About a week later, to my surprise, they called me and asked if I was coming back to work. I couldn't believe it. I was always calling into work or coming in high as a kite, but they never fired me. I was a very hard worker even when I was drunk or high. However, after that episode, I shouldn't have had a job anymore.

Our crack addiction had worsened, and we were spending all the money we had on it. When we ran out of money, we would steal expensive items from a store and return them for a gift card. Then we would trade the gift cards for crack. Since it wasn't cash, we would only get a small percentage worth of crack for what the gift card was actually worth.

Crack is a grim drug. The high doesn't last very long and always leaves a person feeling depressed and wanting more. You could smoke up a half-ounce of it and still not be satisfied.

Our dealer was so spun out that he began thinking bugs were inside his skin. He was always picking at his arms and coming up with new conclusions about where they had come from. He even went as far as to think they were being planted in his dope, so we would all catch them. I always looked at him like he was crazy, but after a stint of being up for days and days, we started to believe it as well. We were hallucinating terribly and started seeing the bugs in our skin, too. That led us to start cutting ourselves with knives and trying to pick them out with tweezers. Samantha and I had become poster board drug addicts.

I had still not been drug tested by my probation officer all this time. I figured I would surely be getting tested anytime, and I had to figure out a way to bypass it. The addiction was so intense that I often thought of ways to get out of having to go in and get drug tested. The ideas I had to avoid getting caught went to the extreme. There were times I wished I had some kind of poisonous snake that I could stick my hand by and get bit, so I would have to be in the hospital. I also thought about jerking the wheel and wrecking my car, anything to keep me from being tested. It's crazy to look back and see how badly drugs alter your reasoning abilities.

Finally, my probation appointment arrived, and I had to devise a fool-proof plan. My dealer referred to the bugs he picked at as scabies. So when I went in, I explained to my probation officer that I thought I had scabies all over me. The plan worked. She freaked out and asked me why I even came into her office. She didn't even want to be near me, so she told me to get out of her office, see a doctor, and tell her when I could come back. I left and never attempted to go to the doctor or anything. I didn't contact her to follow up either. I just wanted to go get high, and I decided I would figure the rest of the plan out later.

About a week passed when I reached a breaking point. We had spent every dime we had, spiraling out of control. I couldn't take the stress anymore, and I told my girlfriend we had to stop living the way we were, but she didn't want to stop. That's when I gave her an ultimatum. She could choose the crack or me. Unfortunately, she chose crack, and our four-year relationship was suddenly over. And to make matters worse, she was now living with the dope dealer. I felt so betrayed and heartbroken, like all my time, effort, and love had been in vain over the past four years.

Sadly, only a few days after the breakup, I was looking to smoke some crack again. Jared delivered it to me, but it was short. He started acting ignorant toward me, and it fueled my anger. A few days later, I was getting drunk and thinking about all the events that had recently taken place. I got myself all worked up and decided I would kill the dope man. He lived about five miles from me down a gravel road in the country. I would go on foot, kick his door in, and then rob and kill him. It was a reckless idea because I knew he kept a 9mm next to him.

I drank a little more and took off walking. I had to cross a highway to get to the gravel road that led to his house. I was really inebriated and had only made it about fifty yards to the highway's edge before deciding to rest for a minute. My head was spinning, and my vision was blurry. I passed out alongside the road and woke up hours later. I had sobered up a little, but I was very tired, so I decided to go back home for the night. Looking back, I know that everything could have ended up so much worse. I am so thankful that God had continued to watch over me, even when I was going down the wrong path.

My probation officer called and wanted to see me not many days after that. When I arrived at her desk, she asked me why I hadn't attempted to see a doctor. She was also irritated that I didn't let her know when I could come back in for a visit. As she continued to talk, I realized that I had been told on by someone. The only people that knew about my plan to avoid drug testing were Samantha and the dope dealer. Someone had told her the whole story about my plan. As a result, I was given several probation violations and was ordered to complete in-patient rehab. She told me that I would not be arrested if I went to rehab.

I was able to get into rehab within a few weeks, and that process was underway. While I was there, I heard that Jared's house had been kicked in by the DEA. He and Samantha were both arrested for drug trafficking crack cocaine. I was so thankful I was in rehab and not there. Although, I still had no intentions of cleaning my life up. I was just doing what I had to do to get by.

After my thirty days in rehab, I was free to go. Still, I needed to visit my probation officer upon release. It was a good feeling to be able to go see her without worrying about getting drug tested or arrested. Little did I know that my troubles were far from over. Everything seemed great when my probation officer came to the waiting room door and called my name with a smile. I didn't notice anything out of the ordinary as I walked to her office, but her tune changed when the door shut behind me. She told me that a warrant had been issued for my arrest, and around the corner, I was met by two police officers.

Even though she told me I could avoid being arrested if I went to in-patient rehab, the court had issued a warrant for my arrest while I was away. I was not a happy camper. After spending three weeks in jail, I was able to get the courts to start my two years of probation over with time served in jail. Even with that, I was nowhere close to being off of probation and right back where I had started.

Not only was I still on probation, but I was now having to attend outpatient rehab, along with going to AA and NA meetings. None of that deterred me, however. I was still using and playing cat and mouse games with the state. It wasn't a matter of if I would get caught, but when.

As time went on, Samantha was bonded out of jail, and we made amends with each other. We were no longer dating, but we were cordial since I was friends with her brothers, Brad and Doug. She and her brother, Brad, stayed at Jared's abandoned home, where the doors had been kicked in. We were all hanging out there getting drunk when one of us mentioned that it would be nice to have some weed, so we began thinking of how to get some.

Our friend, Dan, came to mind. He lived a good distance away, down some very curvy roads with many drop-offs along the edges. Despite being under the influence, we took off on a mission to get some smoke. We arrived at Dan's house and hung out for a while, smoking joints, becoming even more out of our minds, before heading back.

We left in two cars, with Dan driving one car and Brad driving the other. I was riding with Brad, and I remember we were careening down the curvy roads without a care in the world. The last thing I remember is the car driving into the wrong lane and going off the road. Then everything went black.

When I woke up, I was in the ICU, having staples taken out of my head. My mom and brother were standing over me. I was only awake for a few short minutes, and the next time I woke up, I was out of the ICU with a tube pumping blood out of my lungs.

Along the road we had been traveling, there was a huge culvert-like tunnel that a creek ran through. As the tunnel came out from under the road, it opened up except for a big concrete wall on each side. I found out later that we had gone off the road and smashed head-on into this concrete wall, causing the car to get smashed in before flipping. Dan had been driving ahead of us with some of our friends, and they saw the crash in the rearview mirror. They immediately called 911, turned around, and headed back to us.

When they reached the crash scene, Dan started trying to get us out of the vehicle because he thought it was going to catch fire. He later described all the horrible sounds we were making, which ended up scarring him enough that he needed counseling later on down the road. It was not a pretty scene. He managed to get Samantha out, along with me, but Brad was killed upon impact. His side of the car had been smashed in, crushing him.

Dan told me that after he got me out of the car, I started crawling around on the ground, moaning, before I collapsed and became silent. I was no longer responsive after that. It is unclear how long I laid there before EMS arrived. A helicopter had to transport me due to the severity of the crash and how far out in the country we were. Later, I learned that my ribs were broken, causing my lungs to become punctured and ultimately collapse. I was no longer breathing when the emergency personnel arrived. Still, by the grace of God, they were able to revive me on the way to Saint Louis University Hospital.

Thankfully, I was wearing my seatbelt when we crashed. I never wore a seatbelt any other time. It wasn't something I ever cared or thought about, especially if I was under the influence. But for some reason, I had one on that day. The impact was so hard that the seatbelt actually snapped, but it held me back long enough to keep me from going through the windshield. I had a long bruise on my chest from it for almost a year after the incident.

Three weeks elapsed before I was able to leave the hospital. After the crash, I laid in bed for an entire week, unable to move due to the excruciating pain from my broken ribs. Merely clearing my throat brought tears to my eyes. But it was a miracle I was even alive. I should have been dead, and this should have been a wake-up call. Once again, unfortunately, it wasn't. As soon as I was able to get out of bed, I was back to my same old antics, hobbling around in pain but out drinking with my friends.

As I sift through year after year of my life, I can't help but realize how much mercy and grace God has given me. It is truly remarkable.

"It is of the LORD's mercies that we are not consumed, because his compassions fail not. They are new every morning: great is thy faithfulness."
—LAMENTATIONS 3:22-23

It brings to my remembrance something my current pastor said one night at Bible study. "Are we showing as much mercy to others as God has shown to us?" I have found the words of Psalm 136 to ring so true in my life. Truly, His mercy endures forever.

"O give thanks unto the LORD; for he is good: for his mercy endureth for ever."
—PSALM 136:1

"NO GREATER LOVE"

I thank you, Lord
For watching over me,
When I was wretched, blind,
And could not see

So much hurt and grief
I caused my family,
But you knew all that
Way back on Calvary.

You still loved me
While hanging on the cross.
You gave it all
That my soul might not be lost.

You wore the stripes
And thorns to your head.
If not for your mercy,
I'd surely be dead.

Vinegar to drink,
Mingled with gall.
Nailed to a tree,
Knowing I'd fall

Pierced in your side,
And mocked to your face,
Buried in the tomb
That my sins might be erased.

You conquered death,
Rose from the grave,
And gave me your Spirit.
I'm no longer sin's slave.

My life is better
Since the chains have been broke
The road I now walk
Is much easier with your yoke.

My brother's car that hit the house in 2002.

My graduation picture. Troy Buchanan Highschool 2002

CHAPTER SIX

REAPING THE WHIRLWIND

In January 2004, I was nearing the completion of my two years of probation. I had continued using drugs and consuming alcohol for the entire duration of it. Still, I managed to skate by and not get in trouble. However, one day, I received a phone call from the board of probation and parole asking me to come in for a drug test. They told me that I would be put on call-ins if I passed it. This meant I would not have to physically report to see my probation officer. However, if I failed, I would be in trouble and would most likely be going back to jail.

It was a very nerve-racking time because I was definitely not clean. I began drinking pickle juice, vinegar, and water. I took all kinds of cleaner pills. I did anything and everything in an effort not to get a violation. I drank so many liquids that it made me sick. It would have been less of a headache just to stay off drugs.

Then, once I had exhausted all my options, I reported to the office to take my test. I felt so hopeless, knowing there was no chance my test could possibly come back clean. To my amazement, they tested it right there in the office rather than sending it off to the lab, which worked out in my favor. I stood there anxiously, trying to keep my cool and act as if everything was just peachy. I was studying the facial movements of the officer as we waited for the sticks to turn colors. Inside, my heart felt like it would pound out of my chest.

When the results finally showed up, I was stunned. The test came back negative! I wanted to release a wave of emotion, but I had to act as though I was already living a sober lifestyle. It turns out drinking all those liquids paid off. I had successfully flushed out my system. If they had sent it to the lab, they would have tested all my nutrient levels and possibly detected what I had done. However, the onsite test did not.

That day I was put on call-ins. No more visits or anything. I was so excited. I had beat the system! Of course, I had to go celebrate because everything is an excuse to celebrate and use when you are an addict.

A few days later, I went over to one of my coworker's homes to party and play some cards. My friend, Haley, invited a couple of other guys over to join us. When they arrived, I instantly recognized one of them from an ongoing battle that stemmed from the stolen dirt bike incident. He had close ties to the people who told the police about the bike. After I was turned in for the reward money, my brother and Brad, the friend who died in the car wreck, allegedly threw a bowling ball through the window of his vehicle. A pick ax was also put through the hood and into the engine.

A few other things happened relating to this incident, but the latest one was with the guy that had just walked through the door. He had hit my brother in the face with a baseball bat. Ironically, he did not know that I knew who he was or what he looked like. They both came in without any idea of the unhinged events that would soon unfold.

I had already had a bit to drink but kept my composure. Rather than getting heated, I decided to play nice for the moment. I sat there drinking with them, playing cards, offering them cigarettes, and acting like I was their friend. All the while, I was plotting against them in my head. I imagined how I could really seek revenge. I understand now that vengeance is the Lord's (Romans 12:19). However, I had become accustomed to taking matters into my own hands. It didn't matter how much time had passed when someone wronged me; I would wait years for the perfect opportunity to retaliate.

After a few hours of scheming, I was done playing nice. I wanted a piece of them, and I knew my brother would as well. I discretely told Haley what had taken place and that it was going to get ugly. Then I left to go get my brother. I cannot get into all the details, but the police report says my brother and I allegedly kicked the door in and bumrushed them. Later, I found out that my friend had informed the two guys about my plan. When my brother and I arrived back at the house, they were waiting with knives in their hands.

My brother and I were both amped up, so nothing short of being shot with a gun would stop us. It was a very intense fight. They were both brothers as well, so it was brothers against brothers. After one brother was left beaten and lying on the floor, I turned to look towards my brother. The other brother had a knife raised at him while struggling to hold his hands back.

I came up from behind him, grabbed him by the neck, and threw him to the ground. I was slashed in the arm in the process, so once on top, I grabbed the knife by the blade and began hitting him in the face. Meanwhile, Haley was screaming frantically and striking me in the forehead with a hockey stick, trying to get me off of him.

The whole situation had escalated out of control. I had a cut to the arm and a deep gash on my hand. My brother had a stab wound that punctured his lung. One of the brothers was stabbed in the face and beaten severely. The other was beaten repeatedly with an Estwing claw hammer, and both had defecated themselves.

We left the scene and began our drive home. I was pulled over for driving in the wrong lane, not even a mile down the road. When the officer got to my window and saw blood all over the place, he didn't even bother making us get out. He told us to drive to the hospital, and he would follow.

Upon arriving at the hospital, my brother was airlifted to Saint Louis University Hospital. I was stitched up there before being placed in handcuffs and taken to jail. The other brothers had called the police due to fear of their injuries. One of them was absconding from parole, so he was arrested and sent back to prison. It was just one brother and I at the jail, being put on hold while they collected evidence to get a warrant.

Everyone involved refused to write statements and press charges. The police were extremely aggravated with us, but they had to release us the next morning. Between no one wanting to cooperate with the police and there being two sets of brothers, the detectives could not put an accurate case together. It was a complete circus. The police report was in such disarray that there was no way to pursue anyone in court.

I escaped charges that night but later had violations for associating with felons. That was a stipulation of my probation. Therefore, I went from only having to call in once a month to physically reporting to my probation officer twice a week on intense supervision. Having to see her twice a week really didn't faze me like it should have. It was stressful and overwhelming, yet I could tuck it away in the back of my mind when I was in the mood for an escapade. Getting high was always the priority in my life.

Days later, I was hanging with Clyde, the husband of a waitress I worked with. We were drinking beer and decided to smoke some crack. We couldn't get ahold of anyone in town with any, so we drove into the city. In St. Louis, you didn't have to have a hookup. There was always someone standing on the block just waiting for buyers. The only downside is the uncertainty of getting robbed or killed. When I went, I would usually settle off of Goodfellow and Highway 40.

Clyde and I were having a good time drinking beer and getting high. Before long, we had smoked up all our money. His wife, Tina, had a bunch of gifts for someone in the back of the car, so we began going around selling everything there was for more crack.

One of the groups of people we pulled up to while asking for dope wanted to take Clyde into the back alley alone. I honestly did not know if he would make it back, but I waited tight with another guy who stayed back. He told me I needed to keep my windows up and my ride running. He said, "A white boy shouldn't be in these parts of the city, especially in the early morning hours." One person was convinced I was a cop. She said there was no other reason I would have come there since I was white.

Thankfully, Clyde made it back in one piece, and we proceeded with our mobile party. We continued driving around, selling everything we had and getting high. Meanwhile, Tina was blowing up his phone, wondering where we were.

We eventually made it back home around 3:00 or 4:00 in the morning, but we had one problem. All the gifts were gone, and they needed to be replaced. Clyde decided to go into a store and told me to keep the vehicle running. I had no idea as to the extent of what he was getting ready to do. All of a sudden, Clyde came running out with two carts full of merchandise. As he got closer, an employee started to chase after him.

Everything was happening so fast, and he was getting closer by the second. Amazingly, we were able to load up all the merchandise and take off just before he reached Clyde's van. The employee's vehicle must have been parked right by ours because the next thing I knew, we were in a car chase. I was zigzagging all over town, jumping curbs, and going through yards to escape. Since the sun was just about to rise, it was like a ghost town. Had there been an officer in sight, we would have been busted. After an intense high-speed chase, I eventually lost him. We pulled into Clyde's driveway and killed the lights while we sat there, waiting to see if our chaser would cruise by. Tina was furious and scolded both of us for quite a long time.

The sun was starting to give way to another day. I was supposed to be at an outpatient rehab appointment at 8:00 that morning, followed by a visit with my probation officer. I looked horrendous and reeked of alcohol when I arrived to see my counselor. He gave me a breathalyzer test, which I failed horribly, and told me I could not leave until I could blow under a .08, which was the legal limit to avoid a DWI. However, my probation officer said he didn't even want to see me. He just violated me and told me to go home.

It's insane that I went out doing those things the night before, knowing I had to see my drug counselor and probation officer early the next morning. Over time, I racked up more and more probation violations until another warrant was issued for my arrest. This time, I bonded out of jail after a week or so and hired an attorney.

My attorney said it would probably help if my boss came to my court hearing to testify that I was a hard worker and that I was needed on the job. He said this could possibly help me out on the amount of jail time I would receive. While on the stand, my boss was asked how long I could miss work before they would have to fire me. He replied no more than a week.

I thought it all sounded great. For some naive reason, I thought maybe they would only give me a week in jail. The judge took into consideration what my boss said but gave me multiple week-long sentences. The court ordered me to turn myself in once a month for seven days at a time for the entire year. For the next year, I would spend a week a month in jail. It hadn't really worked out as I had hoped for.

My probation also started completely over, and I was still stuck in the system. It was like I was in a revolving door. All I had to do was take a step out, but the life I was living was all I knew. If only I could have seen the wonderful life God intended for me. Maybe then I would have tried to turn my life around.

My brother and I incarcerated together 2004
(me on left, brother on right)

"MY SAVIOR"

This life of sin
Has taken its toll
On my body and mind
As I let the dice roll

So much pain
So much confusion
The world offers peace
But it is just an illusion

There's nothing in it
But the devil's lies
Disappointment and hurt
Painted up like pretty blue skies

I have to get off
This road I'm on
I can see the cliff's edge
And it won't be long

I'm seeking you Lord
Please show me the way
Cleanse this old heart
That is black and grey

Direct my paths
Light my way
Bring me back to the 99
And let me not go astray

Grant me the strength
And courage to be
A living sacrifice
Holy and free

And when the enemy tries

To sift me as wheat

Pray my faith faileth not

And he will flee

Missouri Department of Corrections   Page -   2
Board of Probation and Parole
FIELD VIOLATION REPORT

establishment where alcohol is the primary item for sale. BOUCHER has a
history of alcohol use and has admitted to this officer that he has a
problem with alcohol. The above actions place BOUCHER in violation of
conditions #6, #8.

In response to the above violation BOUCHER stated, "I think they should
just lock me up. I don't know what else to do."

III. OTHER VIOLATIONS

Date	Conditions Violated	Recommendation	Action
3/31/03	#6	Continuance	Continued
1/26/04	#1, #5	Continuance	Continued
2/27/04	#6	Continuance	Continued
3/31/04	#8	Continuance	Continued
4/28/04	#6	Continuance	Continued
5/17/04	#10.1	Continuance	Continued
5/21/04	#6	Continuance	Continued
11/9/04	#8	Continuance	Probation Extended One year
11/19/04	#1, #8	Delayed Action	Continued

IV. RECOMMENDATION

BOUCHER has been in the Intensive Supervision Program since 2/10/04. The
program is designed to be 120 days and BOUCHER has greatly exceeded that
time frame. BOUCHER has been placed in violation status six times for
using illicit substances and/or consuming alcohol since being placed on
Intensive Supervision. BOUCHER has already completed an inpatient
treatment program at Bridgeway on 3/29/04. BOUCHER has been in outpatient
treatment at Bridgeway since 6/15/04. This officer spoke with BOUCHER'S
treatment counselor, Rick Wilson, on 2/22/05 at which time he stated there
was not much more he could do for BOUCHER. This officer has exhausted all
means of aiding BOUCHER in being successful on probation. Therefore this
officer requests that BOUCHER'S probation be Revoked.

V. AVAILABILITY

BOUCHER currently resides at 10 Oak Lane in Troy, Mo., and can be made
immediately available to the Court if so ordered.

Respectfully submitted,

Name: BOUCHER, TERRY   Date -   3/03/0
DOC ID: 1081011   Time -   8:18:3

*Field Violation Report: This shows how many times I violated my
probation in a short period of time. It also states, at the top, where I
said they should just lock me up because I didn't know what else to do.*

CHAPTER SEVEN

ROLLIN' THE DICE

Summer arrived, and my party lifestyle was still racing full speed ahead with no signs of slowing down. My brother, our friend, Grady, and I were doing some drinking at home before heading out to the bar. We wanted to score some crack before going, so we found a hook-up and were on our way.

I wasn't even 21 yet, but they never carded me. However, when we arrived, my brother was already pretty wasted, so they would not let him in by the way he looked. We were really bummed out about that, so we decided to just get some alcohol at the store.

To our dismay, every store my brother tried to get alcohol from refused to sell it to him. I was aggravated because he always seemed to get too drunk to be out in public. We didn't win with the alcohol situation, but we still had our drugs, so we proceeded to a ditch in the alley and smoked up all the crack we had while waiting for my mom to pick us up and take us home.

When we got home, Grady and I wanted to try and get some rest. My mom had fallen asleep on one couch, and Grady was trying to sleep on the other one. I was lying on the living room floor. My brother had been continually nagging my mom to give him a ride into town because he wanted alcohol. I'm not even sure what was going through his mind since it had just been made clear that nobody would sell it to him. Nevertheless, he continued to badger her. We had gotten into a few arguments over it, and I told him he needed to leave her alone.

The last time I told him to stop bothering her, he walked away with a very evil look in his eyes. I shrugged it off and laid back down on the floor to rest. The lights in the living room were off, but a dim light shone on my brother when he came walking back again. He was bouncing off the walls in the hallway as he tried to keep his balance.

While he was stumbling through the living room, he stepped right on me, and after all of his commotion earlier, this set me off. I was enraged and jumped up, punching him and knocking him into the kitchen. We had one of those wooden knife blocks right on the corner of the counter as you entered the kitchen. After gaining his composure, he pulled a butcher knife from the block and began advancing on me quickly.

He started stabbing me rapidly, as fast as he could. It was like he was throwing punches at me, only with a butcher knife. There wasn't much I could do to defend myself except put one of my arms up to prevent him from stabbing me in my major organs. I wasn't feeling any pain with the combination of alcohol, crack, and adrenaline, but I just instinctively started protecting myself.

Eventually, I was able to grab the arm he was swinging with and throw him to the ground. My mom had awakened at the beginning of the brawl when my brother came stumbling into the living room. The light was dim, but she could see what was happening. Her instincts kicked in as well, and she picked up a fireplace poker. In the poor lighting, she thought my brother was on top of me, and she began striking me in the head with the poker.

Despite that, I was able to stop him and get the knife from his hand. I got up and told my mom that we needed to get to the hospital fast, and I rushed out to her car. She ran to get towels to try and stop the bleeding. There was blood everywhere. I was completely soaked in it. Because of this, I had no idea where I had been stabbed. I literally looked like a murder victim out of a horror film. I leaned against the car as I waited for what seemed like an eternity for my mom to come outside. I was becoming lightheaded and began to slide down the side of the car. I knew I was starting to fade out from blood loss and fought to stay awake.

My mom finally came out and tried putting the towels on me as she asked where I was stabbed. I said, "I have no idea, but let's just go! We have to go now!" We took off for the hospital, which was about six miles away. I was telling her to hurry, speed up, don't stop for anything. I didn't know how much time I had.

She flew up to the emergency doors, and I jumped out as the vehicle was still coming to a stop. I came into the lobby looking like I had just taken a blood bath. Everyone looked at me in horror and started asking me what had happened. I began cussing them all out and saying, "What does it look like happened? I was stabbed! Now get me out of this hospital!"

This hospital was infamous for things going wrong, so I did not want my life to be in their hands. I wanted them to airlift me to St. Louis. As I continued to request a helicopter, they started their medical procedures. I'm sure it was very stressful for them. The whole time I was ranting about my brother and criticizing their hospital.

After they had done enough to keep me stable, I was loaded up on a flight to St. Louis University Hospital. The side door of the chopper was open, and I remember just staring down at all the glistening city lights as I seemed to fall into a daze. I'm not sure if they had shot me up with loads of morphine or not, but I was completely at ease as they flew me to St. Louis. There was no more stress and no more panic.

My mom jumped in her car to make the trip to St. Louis as well. On the way, she finally had to stop and wash all the blood off her car. There was so much blood on the side from me leaning against it that she was pulled over twice by the police wanting to know where it all came from.

The sun started to rise as the medical staff sewed up the last stitches on me. The police arrived that morning in my hospital room wanting to ask all sorts of questions. They didn't seem concerned about how I was doing. All they cared about was trying to get me to write a statement. I wasn't very fond of law enforcement, so I didn't really say much, and I also refused to write a statement.

The night of the stabbing, the S.W.A.T. Team went to my home to retrieve my brother. They found him sitting in the hallway smoking a cigarette in complete darkness. He didn't try to resist. They charged him with 1st-degree assault or attempted murder.

I came out with fourteen stab wounds. I was stabbed in the head, butt, back, chest, and arm several times. I had the most stab wounds in my arm because I had raised it in defense, but better my arm than my internal organs. However, I had one stab wound right where my heart was. The doctor said that if it had been just a fraction deeper, I would have been dead in less than a minute. Once again, it was a miracle that I was alive. God had stretched out His loving arms in mercy and saved me from dying in my sins.

Another knife thrust had gone completely through my left bicep and out the other side, cutting many nerves in my arm and bicep in half. They should have done surgery on it, but they gave me a bunch of prescriptions for pain pills instead and sent me on my way. To this day, I still have nerve damage in that arm. The tips of my fingers are always numb and tingly and get cold very easily in the winter, causing them to hurt.

When I was released from the hospital that morning, I busted my huge supply of pain pills open to get high. I began eating and snorting them before taking off on a walk down the road. I had not even been to bed yet since the horrific incident, but I just wanted to go party. It is amazing that after all of that, I was still unfazed by another near-death experience.

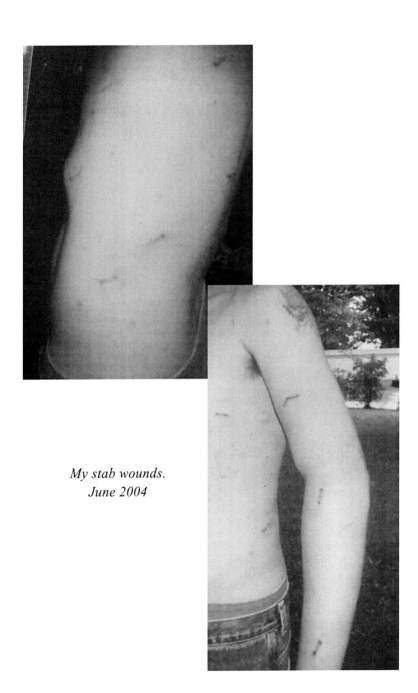

My stab wounds.
June 2004

"CLOSER THAN A BROTHER"

I danced with the devil
And gambled with my life
But you still loved me
And saved me from the knife

How much mercy you have
How much grace you give
You died for me
So that I could live

You were always there
In the good times and bad
Always protecting me
Even when I made you sad

You picked me up
Made the crooked road straight
You were a lamp unto my feet
You guided me to the gate

The gate that is straight
The gate that is narrow
You surely love me more
Than the many sparrows

Thank you for covering me
In the shadow of your wings
For giving me your spirit
So death doth not have a sting

I cannot wait to walk
On the streets of gold
Where there is no more pain
And we'll never grow old

Thank you for your mercy
And all your grace
I look forward to seeing
You face to face

Until that day comes
I'll stick close to your side
And when the arrows come
Behind your shield I'll hide

CHAPTER EIGHT

FUN FOR A SEASON

About a week passed since I had been released from the hospital, and I was due to turn myself into jail to begin my week-a-month commitment. At the time, my brother was kept in a holding cell instead of the general population. Because the story about what happened was on the news, they were unsure how other inmates would react to someone stabbing his own brother. The holding cells were next to booking, so I could see him through a window before I was taken to the general population.

Once I was in population, it didn't take very long for people to see all the stitches on me and question me about what happened. When they found out that I was the stabbing victim they saw on the news, they were shocked, and I began making lots of friends. No one could believe I was still alive and well from what they had heard on the news.

Around the second month of going in for my week-a-month jail sentence, I met a girl named Jenny that I really liked and started dating her. Jenny seemed to have her head on straight, and I never really asked too many questions about what she did for a living. I later found out she was a stripper, not just a normal one, but one with many famous and elite clientele. They ranged from people in Hollywood movies to professional athletes to prominent judges and attorneys. She would leave, and I would get high all night. Then she would come back and throw me a bunch of $100 bills to pay on the restitution I owed for probation. The relationship seemed to be working out in my favor.

Because St. Louis has a federal court house, some jails in the area act as holdovers for federal inmates until they are sentenced. The jail I was at did just that. Because of the high-profile cases that these inmates were often involved in, they painted all the windows black so that no one could see in or out. It may as well have been a dungeon because a person never saw the light of day or knew what was going on outside.

They were supposed to keep the federal and state inmates separated, but they never did. We were all mixed in there together. I didn't complain because the federal inmates had a lot of pull to get things done. All they had to do was write a grievance, and the U.S. Marshalls would be all over it since they were paying big money to have them housed there.

I was friends with many of the federal inmates that were looking at doing lots of time, and there were things they wanted. Since I was always sent to the same place every month, I would take care of them when I came in. It made life easier for them as well as me. They would always call me up the night before and check to make sure I was coming in.

The jail was overcrowded, and many people were forced to sleep on the floor. If they knew I would be there the next morning, they would kick someone out of their bed to make sure I had a bed off the ground to sleep on. It was a win-win for all of us, except for the unlucky one who was kicked out of his bed for me.

I had been coming in for about three months when they decided to move my brother into the general population. The unusual thing is that they put him in the same housing unit that I would always come to. I was glad for it because it gave us time to visit, but I really feel like the staff did it in hopes that we would get into a fight. Due to the severity of the case, we weren't even supposed to be around each other, but it all worked out. Once a month, we visited for a week, played cards, and even smoked and got high together.

I was still up to no good during my time out of jail. One night, I had been drinking pretty heavily, and my mom gave me a ride to Walmart. As I was walking, I spotted someone I had a grudge against. It was rumored that this guy was making fun of the car accident I was in when my friend died. I wasn't very happy with him, but I figured I would catch up with him sooner or later.

As I approached him from behind, I called out his name and told him to stop. He looked back and saw me but continued walking further into the store. I told him to stop a few more times, but I took matters into my own hands when he didn't listen. With his back still towards me, I punched him as hard as I could right in the spine. He dropped to the ground in the middle of the store. People were standing all around us. I heard a few of them saying they saw what I did and would call the police. I decided I better get out of there quick.

Once back in my mom's car, I started asking her for money. I wanted more alcohol, but I had nothing to buy it with. I did have a gift card for Walmart, but I just burned that bridge of opportunity. My mom wouldn't give me any money, even though I was quite persistent in asking. She continued to drive around while I pestered her, but I was very intoxicated and soon fell asleep in the car.

The next time I opened my eyes, an officer was knocking on her car window. She didn't know what to do with me, so she drove me to the police station and asked one of the officers to come out and get me. I spent the night in jail but was released to the streets the following morning.

My brother had a $100,000 cash-only bond for the charges related to stabbing me, as well as numerous other bonds for probation violations. Because of this, there seemed to be no way that he would get out of jail before going to prison. However, my girlfriend was a hustler, and she began to work on things for me. She claimed she struck up a deal with the bondsman; she would go clean his house scantily dressed a certain number of times, and he would bond my brother out.

I wasn't stupid, and I knew there had to be a catch, but I was willing to do whatever it took, as long as it got him back out of jail. The impossible was done. He was bonded out somewhere close to Thanksgiving. Part of his bond stipulation was that we were not to be around each other. We had to be careful about visiting one another, or they could lock him back up.

I found a better job around the six-month mark of my week-a-month jail sentence. This job would not allow me to miss a week, so I was able to get the courts to let me go to jail every weekend for the remaining six months. This worked out for a while but would prove to be way too much stress.

I worked Monday through Friday, got off work, and rushed to get to the jail. Then I would get out Sunday night and start my work week again. On top of that, I also had to see my probation officer twice a week, go to outpatient rehab three nights a week, and have a session with my substance abuse counselor once every two weeks. It was stretching me thin. My counselor wanted to set up a one-on-one visit, and I literally had no free time to do it. I told him the only way I could do it was if he called my probation officer and told her I couldn't come in.

During that time, Jenny became pregnant, and I was actually staying clean because of it. I had to jump through hoops for the state, but I was doing things right for once. Upon getting out of jail one weekend, Jenny said she wasn't feeling good and wanted to know if I could do something with her kids. I took them out to go bowling, so she could get some rest, even though I rarely had any rest with the chaotic schedule I had to endure.

When I arrived home and headed to the bathroom, I found a guy rolling up a blunt of weed. I kept my cool as I talked to Jenny to find out what was going on. We argued about it for a while but then dropped the issue. However, when I returned to the bathroom not even an hour later, I found a gram of cocaine piled up on a dollar bill.

I was absolutely outraged. I had been staying clean, doing the right thing, and then I came home to this. Not to mention she was pregnant. I started to question her, and she said she had suffered a miscarriage, but I really didn't believe her. When I grabbed the drugs to flush them down the toilet, she started hitting me in the face repeatedly.

That broke me. I took off on a warpath out of the house with the cocaine. We were staying in a new development of homes, and there were huge dirt mounds everywhere. I stopped at multiple mounds on the way out of the development, sticking my nose up to the whole pile of cocaine and snorting huge amounts at a time. I had snorted up a gram in a very short time. When I tried calling my mom to come get me out of there, my mouth was so numb from the coke that I couldn't even speak.

High as a kite, I began walking through muddy ditches and water up to my waist, trying to find my way out. I was so high and full of emotions that I couldn't even think. I had been trying to do right for once, and it had all come crashing down around me.

About an hour later, I was finally able to speak well enough to call my mom and ask her to come get me. I would have to see my probation officer soon, but I would fail a drug test, so I turned my phone off for a few days and just hid out. I figured I'd rather have a violation for not coming in than being dirty. However, my plan to clean up didn't last long. I was so upset and hurt by everything that I turned back to the only thing I knew to cope with my emotions. Drugs. I went on a short binge of marijuana, ecstasy, and Xanax.

When I did go back to my probation officer, I had no prepared excuses. I was drug-tested and came up dirty for many drugs. Upon receiving a violation, I was asked if I would like to make a statement to the judge. This time I wasn't trying to make myself look good. I was tired and worn out from playing the game. It was taking a toll on me. In my statement, I told her that I would like to be locked up. I wanted to do the rest of my time in jail and be off probation.

While there are a lot of probation officers that are just waiting for you to mess up so they can send you back to jail or prison, mine was different. For some reason, she liked me and actually wanted to help me. She didn't want to lock me up and kept suggesting that we could try house arrest instead. I told her the truth…that it was just too hard for me to stay clean, and I would end up getting locked up anyway. Despite my admission, she still put in a good recommendation for me, and I continued on probation and doing my weekends in jail.

A few weeks passed before I heard anything from the courts. I was sitting in jail one weekend, waiting in booking to get out, and looking forward to partying with someone I had met. An officer approached me with news that I had a warrant for my arrest. The jail always runs a person's name for warrants upon release to ensure none had been issued since they arrived. Because a new arrest warrant had been issued, I turned my black and white stripes in for orange and was taken into the general population.

My probation was revoked, and I spent the time I had remaining on probation in jail instead. It was bittersweet. On the one hand, I had plans of going to a party and was not expecting to have to stay in jail. On the other hand, this would allow me to come out of jail completely free of probation, and I would have no one telling me what to do.

I spent around three months in jail. Upon being released, I was free from probation and didn't have a care in the world. I decided to hang out with a few friends and a girl named Carmen, who had started coming to visit me while I was in jail. We got high and drank late into the night. Carmen and I got into an argument at the apartment complex at some point in the night. I knew some other people in the same building, so I decided to ditch her and go to the neighbor's place to get some rest.

I was with my friend, Doug, and he had to get to his parole officer in the morning. At about 8:00 A.M., we decided to get going. I wasn't drunk anymore but was pretty hungover when we took off. While cruising down the subdivision, I saw a cop sitting alongside the road. As I passed him, he pulled out right behind me. I kept my head forward and continued to drive the speed limit. It didn't take long for him to flip his lights on and pull me over. I found out later that Carmen had a police officer friend, and she had called him up to wait down the road for us when we left.

When he approached my window, he said he pulled me over for speeding, which I knew was a lie. I said, "I want to see it on your radar." When I challenged him, he said, "I didn't have you clocked, but I paced you going over the speed limit." He then pulled me out of my car and immediately asked me to take a breathalyzer test. I knew I didn't feel drunk, but I also had that nasty aftertaste of alcohol from the night before in my mouth that could possibly be enough to cause me to fail the test.

In Missouri, it was said that it was best to do a refusal to blow when facing your first DWI. You would lose your license for a year, but you wouldn't get a DWI, which could cause more problems in the future. I chose to not blow in his machine, and he wasn't happy about it. Then he decided to do a field sobriety test on me. I know I passed with flying colors. However, the officer absurdly claimed I failed to pivot my foot properly when turning around to walk back to him.

He ended up charging me with a DWI, and I still lost my license for a year. When I went to court, I told the judge I would rather be locked up than be on probation again, but it turned out that I would only be fined since he was a city officer. I also had to complete some classes to get my license back after my year was over. I didn't enjoy having to go to the classes, but I was relieved I was not on probation.

Not long after all that, I went to my mom's place to visit with my brother. While I was there, my neighbor's wife drove by, and my brother started cussing her out as she went past. We never really got along with them, and her husband, Phil, was a deranged meth dealer. She immediately slammed on her brakes and went back to tell her husband.

We were still hanging out in the driveway when her husband came running up on our property, swinging a baseball bat at me. I handled the situation and then took off because part of my brother's bond stipulations was that we were not to be associating with one another. The police ended up finding me and pressed assault charges on me.

Needless to say, I wasn't very pleased with the situation. I asked the officer why I was being charged with assault when my neighbor came on my property swinging a bat at me. The officer then replied that it was because my neighbor was the one who called the cops. I was heated and told him that I didn't realize I needed to call whenever I was defending myself on my own property.

That's when I came to the conclusion that I should leave town. A few weeks prior, I had just gotten out of jail, and I already had two new charges against me. Clyde and Tina had moved south to Branson, so I packed up some of my things and headed there. I got a job doing metal framing right away, but the people I rode with were doing meth all the time. In fact, those foothills were full of meth.

I began snorting and smoking meth just about every day before work. One night, my friends asked me if I had ever shot up. I had never done it before, but they said it was the best high. I thought to myself, "Sure, what could it hurt?" I can still remember it like it was yesterday. Them sticking me. Then seeing the blood draw up into the needle, and then bam! It hit me so hard that I fell to my knees, pouring sweat and vomiting for a long time. My vision went blurry for about five minutes, and I could not see anything. Still, once I got over all of that, I thought it was the best, most intense high I had ever experienced.

I was so high for the next 24 hours that I kept turning down more when they offered it. I couldn't handle anymore. There was a crazy methed-out guy that lived next door, and his wife was always coming over to hang out. We had gone outside to get some fresh air and listen to music when he came out acting nuts. He was obviously as high as a kite and accused me of sleeping with his wife. I had never done anything of the sort, and I began arguing with him.

We went back and forth for a while, but he pulled out a knife and threatened to stab me. I was amped up on meth as well, so I continued to cuss him out and antagonize him. He then retrieved a gun and told me he was going to shoot me. I was feeling pretty invincible, not to mention I'd been through a lot in my life, and his threats didn't scare me. It only made me taunt him more. I told him to pull the trigger. I said it over and over again until he finally lost his nerve and went back inside. Luckily for me, he didn't pull the trigger.

Sometime after that, I was up again all night on meth and drinking. Clyde and Tina took their kids and me to a lake to get some relaxation before going back to work that week. The lake was massive, and there was also a little swim area for the kids. The swim area was roped off by buoys and extended out from the shore about fifty yards. I sat on the beach with a couple of their kids, just drinking and chilling.

There was a little jon boat anchored right next to the buoys of the swim beach. I had never operated a boat before, nor did I know how. Still, I decided to take the boat out to the end of the buoys where my friends were swimming, so I could visit and still bring beer with me. I asked both girls if they wanted to go along. The youngest looked at me like I was crazy and said no, but the other girl, about eight, jumped in without hesitation.

The nose of the boat was facing the beach, and I needed it to face the other direction. As I mentioned, I knew nothing about operating a boat. This one had one of those outboard motors for steering from the back of the boat. I did not realize that whichever way I turned the steering, the boat would go the opposite way. I turned it all the way one way and hit the throttle. I was not expecting the boat to go in the direction it went, and my friend's daughter and I were both thrown out of the boat. The boat's bow was lifted straight up in the air as it raced around us in circles, with the throttle full speed and the rutter in one direction.

There was nothing I could do to stop it. I couldn't jump back in the boat. The entire beach of onlookers just stared in disbelief and horror as the out-of-control boat flew around in the water next to a swim beach full of kids. Finally, after a minute or so, and by the grace of God, the boat somehow straightened out and headed towards a rock embankment away from the beach. The boat plowed into the wall, its propeller continuing to grind noisily against the rocks. If anyone had been unaware of what was going on in the water up to that point, they were certainly aware now.

I was finally able to get to the boat and turn it off. My heart sank as I looked around and saw everyone just standing there staring at me in complete silence. What happened was frightening. Not only could my friend's daughter and I have been cut up and killed by the boat's propellers racing past us, but there were many kids on the beach that could have been plowed over and shredded to pieces as well. That day traumatized me to the point of never wanting to touch a boat again. Unfortunately, it did not make me want to stop using substances. Amazingly, the authorities were never called, and nothing ever came of the situation.

I hadn't planned on coming back home for a while. One of the reasons I left was to hide from the courts, so I could avoid testifying against my brother. However, I ended up being in Branson for only about four months. While I was down there, my brother had gotten into another fight while out on bond. A guy had repeatedly smashed a beer bottle into his face, and he stabbed the guy twenty-two times, all in the upper body. He also stabbed a cop's daughter twice through her arm. She had apparently gotten in the way of them fighting. Because of this, the state really didn't need me to testify anymore. They now had more evidence to help with their case, especially considering he was out on bond for the same crime.

The night I chose to end my stay in Branson, I played with the Ouija board, and the most peculiar thing happened. It told me I needed to call my mom. When I called her, she told me she had just received a subpoena in the mail for me to appear in court for the assault charges on my neighbor. I have no idea why the Ouija board would tell me something I needed to know, but that is exactly what it did. I decided to return home to avoid having another warrant issued for my arrest for failure to appear.

Over the years of going to court, I learned that it was very costly for the courts to have a trial. They would much rather have someone take a plea bargain. Since the state did not want to pay for a trial unless it was a sure-to-win case, I would always push for a trial. The prosecutor would try to make a deal in the meantime, which I would continue to refuse. On the day of the trial, there would be several motions about whether we would be proceeding to trial. During these motions, the prosecutor would try to bargain for a better deal with less time to try and get me to plea out.

Once I had done that two or three times and gotten my sentence as low as I thought possible, I would then snatch up the deal. I can't remember how much time I had to do over the assault on my neighbor, but it was only twenty or thirty days. The price I thought well paid to not have to be on probation.

My brother decided to take a plea deal on both of his charges and received two fifteen-year sentences to run concurrently. He would end up doing over thirteen years of it in prison before being released on parole.

A bizarre ordeal played out with the other two people he had been charged with assaulting. About six months after my brother was sentenced to prison, they were found together in a hotel room on New Year's. She was dead. Shortly thereafter, he ended up hanging himself in the middle of town, in a tree in his parents' yard. Sin never has a good outcome, especially when drugs and alcohol are involved. Sooner or later, the game will come to an end.

"BATTLE READY"

Rejoice not against me
When I fall
For I will rise again
And answer the call

I'll grab my sling
With five stones
And slay my giant
So leave me alone

You have no rule
Or power over me
In the name of Jesus
You must flee

There's no truth in you
You are a liar

And you'll have your time
In the lake of fire

But until then
Get behind me
Keep your chains to yourself
For I am free

Greater is He
That is in me
I will finish the race
And Heaven I'll see

No more pain
No more tears
No more trials
And no more fears

Brothers and Sisters
Keep your heads held high
And don't give up
For the end is nigh

CHAPTER NINE

REPROBATE MIND

I was still going about my life hazardously but had landed a job operating forklifts and cranes loading steal I-beams on trailers. This was a third shift job, so I would usually go to bed in the early afternoon after I had gotten a good buzz on. It put a slight damper on hanging out with people due to my going to sleep during the day. It did not stop my using, however. In fact, I started using alcohol a lot more heavily. My days consisted of getting off work, drinking at least a twelve-pack of beer, and then smoking some weed before going to bed. It took at least all of that for me to even feel a buzz.

On many days, I would drink around twenty-plus beers. I had turned into a very bad alcoholic. Even on the days when I was so tired from work and wanted to come home and just go to bed, I would fight myself to stay awake and drink. After I got a few down, I would start to wake up, and before I knew it, I would be drinking for hours. Many nights, I went into work nearing the point of alcohol poisoning and feeling like death, swearing that I was going straight to bed when I got home. However, as the sun started to rise, I seemed to get my energy back and was ready to do it all over again.

On one of those occasions, I was drinking at my ex-girlfriend, Regan's, house down the road when I met someone who would become my best friend. At the time, Spencer was only around fourteen or so, but he knew how to party, and I commended him for that. He was often either kicked out of school or just didn't go, and we would get wasted together during the day. Most nights, he would swing by so we could smoke some weed together before I left for work.

During this time, I was able to stay under the radar and out of trouble with the law. It is only by the grace of God that I was not in a car wreck of any kind during that time, as I was constantly driving drunk. Every day I would get home, crack a beer open, and start cleaning up from work. I didn't want to waste any time, so I would put shaving cream on my face and shave around my mouth first so I could continue drinking while I finished.

After downing several beers, Spencer and I would usually take a joyride somewhere, often not being able to see straight by the time we headed home. I had taught myself that when I was seeing double, I could close one eye, then focus on the two center lines of the road and drive straight. The two lines in the middle of the other lines were the real ones I needed to follow, and the two outer lines were from the blurred vision.

One weekend, I went to a party at Regan's house. I liked a girl there, but she already had a boyfriend. Before he showed up that night, she told me stories of how he treated her very poorly, even to the point of dumping food on her. It really irritated me, and I could not figure out why she would even be with someone like that.

As the night matured, I became more intoxicated, and my annoyance with the guy grew. We were all out on the deck, and I had decided I couldn't stand him anymore. I told him I wanted to trade punches, but I wanted to do it in the face and not the arm. He and his girlfriend just laughed like I was joking, but I made it clear that I wasn't kidding. I told him I was going to count to ten, and if he didn't hit me in the face, I was going to hit him.

They both continued to laugh at me as I started counting. My ex-girlfriend, Regan, who was standing there also, began to panic as I continued. She frantically started pleading with them to stop laughing and assured them that I was not joking. They ignored her and kept laughing at me. Once I got to ten, I began striking him in the face. I was really drunk, so it was hard for me to stay standing, and we both ended up on the ground. At some point, he smashed a whiskey glass over my forehead, and I was gushing blood everywhere, but I continued to do what I set out to do.

Another friend of mine, who happened to be Regan's boyfriend at the time, finally jumped in and pulled me off. He held me on the ground while both the girl and her boyfriend ran inside and locked the doors. Regan and her boyfriend tried calming me down, and then Regan walked me home. I complied with her, but I was still raging inside. I remember lying in bed, thinking that I would still get him. I thought I would lay there for a while, then go back, kick the door in, and kill him. Thankfully, I passed out.

I woke up to a swollen hand, a cut forehead, and dried blood all over. I was able to go to work, but my hand started turning very red and warm after a few days. I decided to go to the hospital and have an X-ray done. It turns out I had snapped my fourth metacarpal completely in half. I had to have surgery to have a metal rod placed in my hand. The injury didn't slow me down much. Besides the day of surgery, I never missed work and continued with my unruly lifestyle.

Over time, I found some new friends across the street from where I lived, and I began going over there to party after work. Most of them were into speed, and it wasn't long before I started my habit of smoking crack daily again. I was staying up for days with no sleep and going to work high as a kite and delusional. Naturally, this was extremely dangerous, considering I was operating cranes often loaded with 10,000 to 20,000 pounds of steel in the chains. I could have easily killed myself or someone else.

One time, when I was high at work, I hooked up a huge piece of steel plate to an overhead crane that could be operated with a remote and jumped on. I took the remote and flew myself up in the air across the building as though I was taking a magic carpet ride.

In another incident, I caused one of the trucks we hauled trailers with to catch fire in the building. A couple of them ran off propane, and that night, I was using one of those trucks. There was a leak in the tank, so fumes were everywhere, and the truck wouldn't start. I asked a coworker to hook up some chains to drag it out of the building while I steered it. As I was steering the truck, my OCD kicked in, and I just had to try and turn the key once more. When I did this, I heard a WHOOSH! The next thing I knew, flames were shooting up out of the tank a good six feet in the air right next to me. I didn't even think. I just instinctively leapt out the back door, over the fifth wheel and all the tires, and ran away as fast as I could.

The coworker pulling me had no idea what happened until he turned around to see everything up in flames. My boss saw it from a distance and began screaming frantically across the building for me to get a fire extinguisher. I ignored him and continued to run. He was crazy thinking I would try and put that fire out when it could explode at any moment. My coworker continued to remove the truck with the chains as quickly as possible while my boss put the fire out.

Later, when everybody said that something had to have caused a spark to ignite the fumes, I stuck to my story and claimed I hadn't done anything to cause it. Thankfully, no one was injured, but it was a pretty scary situation. It's astonishing to think about all the things that God has saved me from, and I am forever grateful that I'm still alive.

I was never one to miss work, regardless of my using. However, the drugs began to take a toll on me. I began using so much that I started missing work to get high, or I would be too high to possibly contain myself. I started needing to obtain doctor's notes, or I would lose my job. I tried to get a note one night while being strung out. It was the middle of summer, but I had on long sleeves to cover up all the track marks on my arms from shooting up coke. I thought I was fooling the hospital staff, but they weren't stupid. After getting into a huge argument with the people at the hospital, I was forced to leave without a note because I thought I would get the cops called on me.

I used crack cocaine daily for about six to seven months before my binge ended. Those years of my life were very grim. I always pushed it to the limit, mixing different drugs to get a more extreme high. There were many times when I woke up in a daze to see my mom with her hands on me. Later, I found out that she was worried about me and was checking to see if I was still breathing.

I still didn't have any regard for the law. One day, I was cruising down the road towards town to drop someone off when I passed a county cop. I saw his brake lights go on, so I floored it. There was a gravel road just ahead with many turns and routes to travel, and I thought I could lose him. Once I hit the gravel, the dust started going everywhere, and I grew more confident that I would get away. I had been drinking all morning and began throwing beer bottles out during the chase. I traveled for a few miles when I took a wrong turn and came to a dead-end at someone's house. I turned around and was going to try and get out when I saw the officer emerge from the massive cloud of dust.

I was trapped, so I waited for him to approach me. Despite the adrenaline-filled chase, I felt a calm come over me. I knew I was done for, and there was no reason to try to get out of anything. I was drunk, and my back seat was littered with empty alcohol containers. I didn't even try to deny running from him or his accusations that I was throwing bottles out the window throughout our endeavor because he was dead on.

I said that he could just go ahead and take me to jail. He then asked me why I would say that. I explained that I was an alcoholic. Even though I was sober enough to drive due to my tolerance, I knew it only took a couple of beers to blow over the legal limit. To my surprise, the officer was really cool and told me that he would be the judge of that.

Instead of giving me a breathalyzer, which I would have utterly failed, he began doing the field sobriety tests on me. I stood on one foot while counting and then walked so many steps before turning around to precede back towards him. He even shut off the lights that were flashing in my face when I told him they were bothering me. After completing all of his tasks, he informed me that he would let me go if I dropped my friend off in town and went straight home. I was absolutely stunned and showed him a lot of gratitude before going on my way. I was spared once again, which didn't help me wake up to reality.

I was back to the normal routine of drinking and smoking marijuana. One day, Spencer and I found ourselves needing some more weed. I decided I was not going to drive to get it that day. Due to my recent run-in with the law, I thought it would be best to find someone else to take us.

After searching for a ride for some time, I finally got ahold of my waitress friend, Haley, from the pizza place I used to work at. Haley said she would drive, but we would have to get to town where she was. I decided to have Spencer drive to town, and then Haley could drive from there to the drug dealer's house.

The entire time Haley drove us, she persistently asked me to go into the pharmacy and purchase some pseudoephedrine for her. The pills were used to make meth, but a person could only buy a couple boxes a month. All I wanted to do was get some weed and get home, so I continued to tell her no.

After denying her enough times, she turned to another friend riding with us and asked him. He gave in and said yes, but he was barely eighteen and had no clue what he was doing. I decided I would just go in and get the pills for her.

I purchased them and was on my way out without a care in the world besides wanting to get high. I was almost to my car when the county's D.E.A. came swarming around me with guns drawn, telling me to get on the hood of the car. It was all surreal, like something straight out of a movie. I couldn't believe what was happening. While I was pinned face down on the hood of my car, I heard Haley call one of the officers by his first name like she had a relationship with him. I gave her an evil stare through the windshield as cuffs were placed on me, and my rights were being read.

The officers said they had kicked her door in and found a meth lab there. I told them I had no idea about all that, which I didn't. All I wanted to do was smoke some weed. Once down at the station, the cops did what they always did and tried to get a confession out of me, but I didn't have anything to confess about. I didn't know about the meth lab, and I had no intentions of making any meth.

After not being able to get anything out of me for a confession, the officer then started asking what I could do to help myself. In other words, what he meant was who could I snitch on. In my mind, I knew that was never going to happen. I'd go do time before opening my mouth about anything I knew. But I played it off as though I was considering working with him. I figured it would make him a little easier to deal with. If he thought I would help him out, he might be more lenient on me for the time being.

I told him I knew some stuff but wasn't sure how much I wanted to share and would have to think about it. To my amazement, the plan worked better than I thought it would. He decided to let me go with no bail. I was just booked and released. Then I asked for his card and said that I would be in touch soon, and I called my mom to come get me. I was out of there in no time.

My mom stopped to get gas about a mile from the police station, and wouldn't you know, that same cop pulled up as I was pumping the gas. Since I was already out of jail, I decided to let him in on the secret that I wouldn't be helping him out. Smirking smugly, I told him I understood how it all works and that I would be expecting a warrant for my arrest soon.

Getting out before my warrant was issued gave me time to get my affairs in order. I had a 401(k) at my steel-loading job, so I quit there to get my money. I needed the money to post my upcoming bond, as well as hire an attorney, and that was the only way I could collect all of it. In the meantime, I continued on with my unstable lifestyle. There was nothing new under the sun.

One evening, some friends and I were hanging out at an old, abandoned rock quarry. It was like a massive cave with many corridors, and a little stream ran through it. One section opened up to a huge body of water, surrounded by sheer rock walls. We enjoyed climbing to the top and jumping off the cliffs, often while very intoxicated. It is a miracle that none of us ever fell from those cliffs or failed to jump out far enough, causing us to hit the rocks below.

I actually lived in this cave for a couple of weeks at one point in my life. I had been kicked out of the house, and it seemed like a nice, secluded spot to party it up. Some friends and I had a bonfire one night at this rock quarry and were doing some drinking. In order to get there, we had to cross railroad tracks, barbed wire fences, and many no trespassing signs. We never paid attention to any of that, though. We just did what we wanted to do.

In the middle of our evening, we were interrupted by an officer on a megaphone, ordering us to come out immediately. First, he threatened to have my car towed if we did not comply, but we were all drunk, and the two girls with us weren't of age to be drinking. After several attempts to get us to come out, the officer then proceeded to tell us that if we did not come out, he would send the dogs in to get us. That didn't faze us either. We moved farther into the cave and climbed up a rock wall hidden in the dark and out of reach of any dogs.

Finally, after many threats, the officers came in to start their search. We were quite far back, and what had been a rock floor had turned into deep, sinking mud. We could hear them getting closer and see the light from their flashlights. When it looked like they were just about to give up, their lights just barely caught some of our belongings that we had dropped in our attempt to hide. The officer then followed our tracks with his light right up to where we were hiding.

Immediately, he pulled out his gun and started yelling at us to get our hands up. Then he told us to walk down backwards. I don't know what he was thinking or how he expected us to come down a rock wall backward with no hands, but we did our best in hopes of not being shot. All I could think about was one of my friends, Mikey (who we used to terrorize the neighborhood with), who had been shot in the head through the back glass of his vehicle by an officer from the same department.

Once back at the police car, he told us he thought we were making meth due to receiving numerous, recent calls about it. They asked many questions, but we weren't very cooperative. We didn't really care what they had to say, and the girls kept asking the officers to get their Little Debbie snack cakes from the car.

When it was all said and done, they took my friend, Doug, and me to jail and gave the girls a ride home. We were drunk and, in the mood, to raise cane. Many things in that jail were illegal, from not having the federal inmates separate from the state inmates to having people sleep on the floor. We used all of this to our advantage.

We began cussing them out, telling them that we would contact the news and the United States Marshalls and have their jail shut down. I screamed at the correction officers until I blacked out and fell asleep. I woke up in the visiting room instead of a holding cell. I guess they thought I was too riled up to put me in with the other inmates. At the end of the whole ordeal, my friend and I both walked out of jail the next morning without a single charge for trespassing, verbal assault, or contributing alcohol to minors.

There was never really a dull moment in my life. Not too much time had elapsed since the rock quarry incident, and Doug and I were off on another adventure. We weren't far from the Mississippi River and would go tubing and fishing from time to time. This time, we decided to go camping on an island in the middle of the river. We packed up our stuff, and his dad took us there on his boat, with a Jet Ski tied to the back for us to use later.

Upon arriving at the island, we told his dad that we would stay for a few days but would get ahold of him when we wanted to be picked back up. Then we set up camp and took the Jet Ski to the marina a few miles upriver to get more supplies. We got no more than 20 yards from the island's shore when the Jet Ski broke down. We had to jump off and guide it back to the beach, but there was no fixing it. With no cell phone reception, getting to the marina was our lifeline, and now we no longer had that. We drank some beer that night and hoped for a solution the next day.

However, the next day didn't start off any better. We were both hungover and dehydrated, and all we had to drink was warm beer. We didn't pack any water, but we did have two thirty packs of beer, so we continued to drink that. The Mississippi River was extremely wide, so when we tried signaling to people for help, they were just too far away.

By the next day, we were both feeling really bad. As the day progressed, we no longer had the strength to stand on the shore and try to signal for help. We just laid in our tent out of the sun, hoping for someone to stumble upon us, although the odds of that happening seemed pretty slim. Many times we thought we heard a boat getting really close, as though they were going to stop, only to lift our heads and see them pass on by and then disappear into the distance.

We were on our third day with no water, and it felt like we were on the verge of dying. It was midmorning, and we thought we heard a boat pulling up to the beach. Because we had heard this so many times before, only to be let down, we didn't think too much of it. However, this time it really was somebody pulling up to the island. Doug's mom, Rachel, had finally come looking for us since no one could get through to us on our cell phones. It was a miracle.

We struggled to make our way to the boat. We were so weak that we could barely stand and desperately wanted some water. Disappointingly, the only thing to drink on the boat was Mountain Dew. It was not what we wanted or needed, but at least it was cold. The ride back to land felt like an eternity. I have never wanted a sip of water so badly in my entire life.

It was a terrible experience, but we lived through it. A little longer on that island, and I don't believe I would be writing about it. However, after being rescued, Doug went into a diabetic coma and almost died the following day. Apparently, the doctors said he was already borderline, which was triggered by our recent fiasco. Luckily, he made it through. Although sadly, he is no longer alive due to his drug use and lifestyle.

Oh, how I wish I would have reached out to God sooner, that I would have realized there is so much more to life than all of the pain and hurt…that Jesus was right there waiting for me the whole time. He is waiting for you as well…waiting for you to take a step of faith, waiting for you to give him permission to transform your life.

"TRASH TO TREASURE"

God is searching
For the broken in heart
The ones beat down
And torn apart

The ones in pieces
And left all alone
Having no friends
And no one to phone

For the one who thinks
There has to be more
He is right outside
Knocking at your door

He is the horn of salvation
And our strong tower
He holds in His hands
All might and power

To change your life
To turn it around
To put your feet back
On solid ground

Are you going to get up?
Will you answer the call
Jesus still loves you
No matter how much you fall

Grab God's word
For it is the meat
To rescue you from
These lonesome streets

All you have to do
Is trust and believe
Just keep asking
And you shall receive

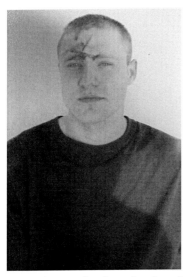

The aftermath of my forehead after having the whiskey glass smashed on my head.

The steel plate I took ride on at work. Approximately in 2008.

This is the opening to the cave where we partied.

CHAPTER TEN

BAD TRIPS

Two weeks after the pseudoephedrine pill incident, I found out a warrant was issued for my arrest. I wasn't concerned because I was able to cash in my 401(k) money prior to it. My friend, Rachel, gave me a ride to the jail, and I turned myself in with all the money I needed to bond right back out. I was in and out within an hour.

Then I went on another party binge. I didn't even attempt to get another job because I knew that I could potentially be locked back up. Spencer and I would pick up a couple of ounces of weed a day, sell half of it, and smoke the other half for free. We did this for at least a few months.

I also began doing a lot of cocaine again. Doug had a good drug hookup, and with him being a diabetic, I had access to as many clean needles as I wanted. One night, I did a massive shot of coke and was on the floor throwing my guts up. I was so sick that I threw my needle in the trash and said I was never shooting up again.

We must not have had any extra needles on us that night because once my high wore off a little, I did the unthinkable and dug my needle back out of the trash to do another shot of cocaine. Thankfully, it wasn't contaminated. I always put the cap back on the needle when I threw it away, so nobody could accidentally get pricked. But the idea of stooping that low to pull a needle back out of the trash to get high would've been unimaginable to me when I smoked my first cigarette or when I began "just smoking some weed."

During this time, Doug and I decided to attend an annual hippie festival called Schwagstock held in the southern boot hills of Missouri. It was held in Salem and was very much like Woodstock, only on all privately owned land. A lot of happy-go-lucky kinds of people attended Schwagstock. Drug peddlers would walk around shouting out which drug they were selling like someone selling hot dogs at a ballpark. There was an abundance of marijuana and opium and every hallucinogenic drug you could think of.

We bought some LSD not long after arriving. I took a couple of hits and decided to save the other two for home. We spent most of the night walking around in a haze, meeting new people, and smoking weed and opium. There were people spinning glow sticks and people beating drums around a massive bonfire. Some were spinning fire on ropes. Eventually, the night came to an end, and the sun began to peek its head up over the forest.

I was becoming hungry and running out of cigarettes, and I hadn't packed anything. Though I wasn't sober, I thought I was okay enough to drive. My high was almost gone, and I had not drunk any alcohol like Doug had, but he insisted on driving, so I didn't argue.

We weren't even a half-mile down the road when we saw a state patrol tailing us. Before long, his lights were flashing, and we were being pulled over. I still had the two hits of LSD wrapped in cellophane that I was trying to get out and eat. I almost couldn't find them because they were clear with what looked like a tiny microchip board on the inside. The officer was almost to the window when I finally found them and ate them.

One of the first things he asked us was if we had any shrooms. We felt like it was entrapment. They were aware of what went on at the festival, and they just waited for people to leave the festival so they could pull them over. We didn't have anything on us anymore, so we were clean, except Doug had been drinking, and I had just eaten another two hits of LSD.

They got Doug out and gave him a breathalyzer test, which he failed. We sat there for quite a bit of time while they searched the vehicle and waited for information to come back over the radio, etc., and I was starting to feel really high. I remember gazing in the mirror and being mesmerized by the officer's lights flashing.

They issued Doug a DWI and told me I needed to drive. I played it cool to the best of my ability and then slowly pulled the car away from the scene. I was about to set off on a very dangerous drive. LSD is not a drug somebody wants to or should drive on, especially in the boot hills of Missouri. Everything looks like it's moving, breathing, and blowing in the wind when you're high on it. On top of that, all the roads in that area are hilly, snaky, and without a shoulder. There are only trees right next to the road or very deep drop-offs on the side of mini-mountains.

As I drove, I felt like I was on a rollercoaster going up, down, and around as my hands stayed clenched to the steering wheel. We became lost in the hills and started running out of gas. I drove without any sign of getting closer to civilization for miles and miles. My mind was racing a hundred miles an hour, and I was drawing close to a full-blown panic. Finally, we saw a house up in the distance, and there were a couple of people outside in the yard.

I knew that I was a wreck and didn't really want to have any interaction with other people. However, I didn't have a choice. We needed help. I stopped at the house and got out of the car to approach the people. I'm sure my pupils were the size of pennies, and they had to have known I was on something. I explained that we were lost, but it is very difficult to talk while on LSD. You often know what to say, but you just cannot get it to come out of your mouth. Other times, a person can forget what they were talking about in the middle of a sentence. The mind on LSD is completely scattered.

They brought out a map to try to explain to me where I was. I acted like I understood what they were saying, but I was out of my mind. All the lines on the map were moving around every which way, but I thanked them for their help, and we were on our way.

All I could remember was something about turning when I got to a T in the road, but I couldn't remember if I was supposed to turn left or right. We eventually came to the T the guy was talking about; however, I still had no idea which way to go. It was literally in the middle of nowhere. There was nothing around...no people, no traffic, just absolutely desolate. I sat there for what seemed like fifteen to twenty minutes, spaced out and pondering which way I should go. I couldn't afford to make the wrong decision. We were almost out of gas.

As I sat there staring through the windshield, a vehicle pulled up alongside me. It happened to be the same people that tried to help us. They pointed me in the right direction, and finally, we were on our way with a little hope that we just might make it out of the hills.

We finally made it to a gas station and got directions as to which way to head next. In the process of being lost, we had driven along the southern border of Missouri, from one side to the other. We now realized that we needed to drive straight north, up half the state, to get back to Saint Louis. I am not sure how I was able to keep my composure and not fall into a massively bad trip. With all the woods around us and the trees swaying back and forth, it seemed as if we were lost in the deepest part of the jungle.

We managed to make it back home in the evening with no wrecks or further run-ins with the law. I was pretty much sober by the time we pulled into the driveway. That was truly one of the worst experiences I ever had with drugs, and I would never want to relive it. Once back,

I did some drinking to calm down because my nerves were shot. I had not learned anything from my death-defying drive.

I hired an attorney for my pending case but continued to stay on the same path. About a month after going to the festival, Spencer and I were on a search to get a quarter-pound of weed. We made some calls, and one of our regular dealers had enough, so we headed over to the next town where he was. Before we arrived, though, we found out that a friend of my cousin, Pat, could get it to us much cheaper. We were almost at our dealer's place, so we debated a little about what to do.

Going against our better judgment, we decided to go with the cheaper option, even though it was over an hour away. Spencer and I picked up my cousin, Pat, his friend Randy, and Randy's girlfriend before setting out on our mission to this unknown source. Since I had never dealt with this guy before, I gave Randy a digital scale to weigh the purchase and told him that now that he had the scale, it had better not be short because if it was, it would be on him. Once we were down the road from the guy's place, we dropped Randy off to do the deal and circled the area a few times, waiting for him to come out.

Once he got back into the car, I was immediately irritated. The weed was in a Wonder Bread bag, and it did not look anywhere near the amount it should be. I put it on the scale, and sure enough, it was only half of what it should have been with the huge bread bag. My anger rose quickly as I began interrogating him. Since I had been drinking, his girlfriend had been driving, and I was riding in the back seat. Before the car started moving, I grabbed Randy around the neck from behind his seat, but because the car was stopped, he and his girlfriend were able to jump out and get away.

At this point, I was livid. I jumped into the driver's seat to find him but was unsuccessful, so I took off for home. We were up in Northern Missouri, not too far from the state line, in an unfamiliar area. Due to my anger and being under the influence, I took the wrong highway without noticing. I was unknowingly on my way to Illinois.

I cracked open a beer and zoomed down the highway in a rage. I hadn't been on the highway too long when I saw a highway patrol sitting in the median as I blew past. Immediately, he hit his lights and took chase. I instinctively threw my beer out the window before he caught up to me and told Spencer to throw the weed out the window, but he was still holding onto it as the cop car approached us. When he did finally throw it out, the officer's bright lights had my car lit up, and we found out later that it was all on film, coming out the window and skipping down the highway.

It was game over. I pulled off to the shoulder and waited for an officer to come to the window. One officer came and began asking questions, while another went and retrieved the Wonder Bread bag of marijuana. All of us in the car kept our mouths shut until we realized they had video footage. Still, I continued to keep my mouth shut about the weed because it was seen coming out the passenger window.

I was asked to step out of the vehicle, and at that point, I didn't care anymore. I had gone from raging mad to no regard. I knew I would fail a breathalyzer, so I told the officer he could just take me to jail. There was no sense in going through all of it. But he told me he wanted to do a field sobriety test.

I remember going through the ABCs like he asked me to, and when I got to the end, I began singing, "Now, I know my ABCs. Next time, won't you sing with me?" as I just laughed. I was very cooperative as I was being placed in cuffs. The police report actually said that I was very indifferent and friendly.

They would later give me a breathalyzer test. It registered at .181 BAC. According to statistics, most people experience blackouts at a .2 BAC. However, I was pretty much perfectly coherent and remember the entire ordeal.

Pat, Spencer, and I were all taken to the closest police station. Pat was free to go once a ride came for him. Spencer, who was a minor, took the possession charge and digital scale charge for me since it would have sent me to prison, and he would only get sent to juvenile for a bit.

The police officers were surprisingly merciful. I knew that anything under 35 grams of marijuana would be a misdemeanor instead of a felony, so I told them that the Wonder Bread bag weighed a lot. There was a good chance that it might not be enough for a felony charge. Since we had all been laid back and cooperative up to that point, the officers took all the weed out of the bag and put it on my scale to see if it was under 35 grams. It wasn't.

I was charged with my second DWI. My mom came and posted my bond, but now I had two pending charges. After going to court a few times on the DWI, I told my attorney that I just wanted to do some time and get it over with.

On the day of my sentencing, I stood in front of the judge as he asked the prosecutor if it was my first DWI offense. I knew it was my second, but I kept my mouth shut because he was not talking to me. But evidently, the prosecuting attorney had not done her homework on me. She looked at all her paperwork as if she knew what she was doing and told the judge it was my first time. I could not believe what I was hearing. They offered me thirty days in jail, which I happily accepted. I could do thirty days standing on my head.

Pat and I owned tattoo guns, and I knew that every time a person goes to jail, they have their tattoos documented. So I decided to make my resentment against law enforcement evident by giving myself a fresh tattoo on my leg that said: "(expletive) the law." It had an anarchy symbol around the word "law" and the police code for killing cops right below the anarchy sign. I sure was proud and eager for them to see my newest tattoo. It was my way of cussing them without getting a new charge.

Before turning myself in, I rolled up a fat joint and taped it to the bottom of my coffee table. That way, I would be able to catch a buzz as soon as I was released. Thirty days went by with ease, and I was back out on the streets. Although I managed to skate by with minimal jail time, I reaped the consequences of a second DWI and lost my license for five years.

In the meantime, I was still dealing with my charge from the pills at Walgreens. I was pushing for trial since I was charged with possession of a precursor drug with intent to manufacture methamphetamine but had no intentions of making any meth. I had already paid my attorney to go to trial, but as the trial drew nearer, my attorney suddenly started sounding like he was on the prosecutor's side. He would say things like I "knew what it was going to be used for." I was appalled at what I was hearing. I had paid him a lot of money to defend me, and now it sounded like he had made some kind of deal with the prosecutor, and I was going to get railroaded.

If my attorney really had decided to help the prosecutor (which he used to be himself), then I could end up getting seven years in prison. I didn't feel good about it at all and had all kinds of thoughts running through my mind. After weighing out the few options I had, I decided to take a plea deal for two years' probation. That was not what I wanted to do. I had told myself that I would never choose to do probation again. I had even gone to the Army recruiting office to see if they would let me join. If joining the military could get my charges dropped, I thought it might be worth a shot and even help me turn my life around.

After meeting with the recruiter, however, I realized that I couldn't even volunteer to die for my country because of my criminal record. I chose to do probation and decided that I would just have to stay clean and get my life together for once. But I was only kidding myself. I was not ready to change, even if it meant going to prison. It would take a few more setbacks before I finally surrendered my life to God.

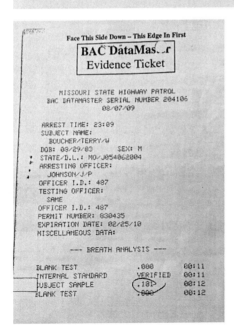

My second DWI after the Wonder Bread bag of marijuana incident and when I started to sing at the end of my ABC's during field sobriety test. August 2009

"SOBER AND VIGILANT"

Put on your armor
And fight for the Lord
Bind together
Make a threefold cord

Guard your heart
Pick up your shield
Grab your sword
And get to the field

There's a battle raging
A fight for our souls
To lock us away
With hell's hot coals

We mustn't grow weary
Or start to slum
For we know not when
The Lord will come

He'll come in the clouds
At the twinkling of an eye
He will quicken our bodies
So that we cannot die

We'll be raptured up
To the heavens above
Surrounded by glory
And God's perfect love

The pain on earth
Will not compare
To seeing the one
Who numbered our hairs

So trim your lamps
And look to the East
For the bridegroom to come
And invite you to the feast

Me with my snake friend.
November 24th, 2007

CHAPTER ELEVEN

NOTHING CHANGES IF NOTHING CHANGES

Instead of my life changing for the better after taking the plea deal, it progressively worsened. Because I was about to start my probation, I figured I had better do drugs while I had the chance. A bunch of us decided to get together and throw one last party before I had to stay on the straight and narrow.

One of my friends had some raw heroin in his possession at the party. That was one drug I had told myself I would never do. I had been locked up with people in jail and rehab who were going through withdrawals from it, and they looked like absolute death. They acted as if they would rather die than go through the agony they were feeling. But despite what I had always told myself, I decided to try it just once.

When they gave me the heroin, they told me to do the whole amount, but I didn't have a good feeling about it. Raw heroin is extremely potent, so I decided to do just half of it instead of taking the full amount they gave me. Within minutes of taking the drug, I started feeling terrible and abandoned the party to go inside. It was a struggle just to stay upright.

It wasn't long before my vision began to blur, and I started nodding out. Every time I would open my eyes back up, I couldn't see straight. After what seemed like forever, my vision would correct itself, but

I'd be nodding back off by the time I could see again. I started getting very hot and sweating profusely. I was so hot that I stripped down to my boxers.

I had done numerous drugs over my life, but I knew what I was experiencing wasn't good at all. Having had friends who had overdosed on heroin, as well as on fentanyl, I knew the risks of consuming it. The thought crossed my mind to call 911 because I felt like I could be dying. I didn't know what to do because I certainly didn't want to die, but at the same time, I didn't want to get arrested either. Instead of calling 911, I just sat there for a good hour, pouring sweat and trying to keep myself awake, riding it out in hopes I would come down enough to stay alive.

Thankfully, I did eventually come through without overdosing. Had I done the full amount like they suggested, there is no doubt in my mind that I would have been dead. I would have fallen asleep, never to wake up again. The next morning, I decided I would do much less of it, and through the course of that year, I did heroin maybe another five or six times but never got to the point that I went through withdrawals.

Shortly after this experience, I met with my probation officer for the first time. Surprisingly, she said that she didn't care if I drank alcohol. That was very odd because usually, no matter the reason a person is on parole or probation, they make it a stipulation that you cannot drink.

I took her permission to drink and ran with it. Over the next year, I became very addicted to alcohol. During this time, I stuck to drinking and doing synthetic drugs that wouldn't show up on a drug test, like bath salts or fake weed. Those drugs were a gamble, though, because you never really knew what was in them. They were just a bunch of chemicals mixed together to get you high.

Many people lose their minds on synthetic drugs, running around completely naked, attacking people, and even eating their victims' flesh. My cousin, Pat, ended up flipping out on bath salts. He was arrested after holding his family hostage inside with a shotgun. A totally naked maniac, he threatened to burn the house down with everyone in it. Thankfully, nothing like that ever happened to me while I was using them.

Another drug I was introduced to during this time was a new drug out on the streets called Bliss. My friends and I had no idea what it was or what it was like, but once we heard about it, we just had to try it. We knew about a guy who had tons of it, along with ecstasy and LSD, so we made a call to have it delivered to us on an old gravel road. Although we made the order sound legit, we had no intentions of paying for anything. That night, we robbed the dealer of hundreds of dollars' worth of LSD, ecstasy, and the new Bliss drug.

We all partied like it was the turn of the century that night. The Bliss was unlike anything I had ever done. It was like a mix of all drugs and felt like one big roller coaster ride with a lot of ups and downs. I justified doing all these drugs because they did not stay in my system for very long.

The binge went on for days. We were partying in a tent I had put out in my front yard. After going days with no sleep, I fell asleep in the tent early one morning. When I woke up, I found my probation officer's business card on my front door. She had shown up at my place while I was asleep. Had she decided to come check out the tent, she would've seen the mirrors with lines of powder everywhere that were lying right next to me, and I would have been arrested. However, once again, I had barely escaped my lies.

Later that day, I reported to her and explained that the tent was just a drinking party. She didn't look much into it, and I was free to go about my business. Further into that week, my friends and I were doing some ecstasy, among other things (that I can't write about), next to the highway. It had gotten someone's attention, and the police were called, but we were unaware of it at the time.

Sometime after midnight, while we were chilling on a trampoline and drinking in my front yard, we saw a cop coming down the road with a spotlight searching yards. The light made its way right to us, and we were spotted. None of us even said a word. We all just instinctively jumped up and took off running. Spencer and his girlfriend, Teagan, were in front of me, and I trailed behind, carrying a case of beer. The cop busted a turn and started flying right through my yard. I was high as a kite, and with the flashing lights, it felt like I was in an arcade game. I had no time to think and just told myself to run and don't look back.

We made it behind my house to where a metal fence covered part of the backyard. My friends were heading straight for it, and I tried to warn them, but it was too late. Spencer's girlfriend smashed right into the fence, but Spencer never even stopped. He continued heading towards the woods a few hundred yards away while the police car continued chasing him, tearing up everyone's yards in the process.

I jumped a different fence and zigzagged my way to safety. While waiting for the cops to leave, I decided to sit in the woods and drink beer. I kept thinking the cops would come back to my house since that was where the chase began, but they never did return. Both of my friends had been caught, but once again, I had escaped. I found out later that Spencer heard an officer radio to another saying, "There's still one out there." Spencer just laughed and said, "Good luck," knowing I was on my own turf and already long gone.

In the meantime, my cousin, Pat, and another guy named Guss had gotten into cooking meth. I normally wouldn't have had a problem with it. However, my cousin's wife called me one day, scared and not knowing what to do. She said they had been cooking meth in the house for days and had been giving each other tattoos. The whole house was so full of fumes that she and her kid couldn't breathe.

I told her I would take care of it and asked her to put Pat on the phone. I lived only a few miles away and said I would be on my way in a few minutes. I told him if Guss was not gone by the time I got there, he would be very sorry.

Spencer and I grabbed a few beers and started our journey down the highway on foot. I asked my cousin if the guy was still there when we arrived. He said he wasn't, but I didn't believe him and began checking every room and closet. I didn't find him, but I had a feeling he wasn't far away. He was a dope head who had burnt all his bridges, so he didn't have anywhere else to go. I knew he probably hadn't gone far and thought maybe he was hiding nearby in the woods or tall grass.

I decided to drink for a while and go back out when he wouldn't be expecting it. A few hours later, I grabbed a knife and searched for him outside. I saw many areas where the grass had been knocked down, so I knew he had been out there, but my search was fruitless.

I had given up the search and headed back to the house when I passed a little jon boat. Even though I thought it was highly unlikely that he'd hide so close to the house, I decided to take a peek anyway. Sure enough, there he was, fast asleep on the boat's floor.

Quietly, I went back into the house and told my cousin I had found him. I planned on beating him thoroughly. At first, I put a canned good in a pillow case, thinking it would make a great weapon, but I realized I could get too carried away and things might turn out bad. I decided my fists would have to do.

Back outside, I stood over the sleeping man, trying to decide how I was going to proceed. Finally, I decided just to go for it. I raised my hands and started blasting him. He woke up in a daze while being battered. Rolling out of the boat, he scrambled frantically onto his feet, pleading with me not to hurt him.

He began walking backwards to try to put some distance between us. I told him to come closer, but he wouldn't comply, so I grabbed all of the little belongings he had and threw them on the ground. Then I soaked them in gasoline and set them on fire right in front of him. With that, I warned him to never come back, or he would pay immensely.

I had committed yet another senseless act that there was just no excuse for. Though I was under supervision and supposed to be changing my life for the better, nothing had changed. I was doing the same things over and over, expecting different results, which is what rehab facilities would describe as insanity. The fact is that nothing will change unless changes are made.

If your life is out of control, and you want it to change for the better, then everything needs to change. This includes people, places, and things. Everywhere you go, everything you do, and everyone you associate with. If you do not change all of this, sooner or later you'll fall back into the same pit you have always been trapped in. I wish I had taken the initiative during that time to become a productive person in society, but I just continued down the same path of despair.

"NEWNESS OF LIFE"

My old life
And wretched choices
Bound me in chains
And hearing voices

I walked away
And pushed you aside
Then the devil pulled up
And took me for a ride

I ran the streets
Searching for a high
Having a death wish
Not caring if I died

He lied to me
And said it would be fun
Warrants for my arrest
Now I'm on the run

What is my life
But a vapor in the wind
The party won't last forever
And will soon come to an end

But You are the potter
And I was the clay
Your hands were on my life
Each and every day

Your forgiveness is greater
Than East is to West
You've seen me through
The trials and tests

You gave back the years
The locusts had ate
Covered me with your blood
And gave me a clean slate

CHAPTER TWELVE

LIFE IN PRISON?

Sometime near the end of 2010, my friends and I had a bonfire in my backyard. One of them brought over a girl named Abbie. It turns out she was someone I had ridden the bus with in grade school, but we had never really conversed before. We hit it off pretty well that night and started dating shortly after that. This set in motion a chain of events that would alter my life forever.

I found out that Abbie's dad was also the bondsman that my ex-girlfriend, Jenny, had gotten to bond my brother out of jail. He and I had also been in some arguments in the past. He had threatened to revoke my brother's bond, which I didn't appreciate. As a result, I had made some nasty promises to him. Considering he and I didn't necessarily see eye to eye, dating his daughter probably wasn't the most ideal situation for me to be in.

However, the relationship seemed great at first. I was drinking all day, every day, which most girls would not appreciate, but Abbie was addicted to heroin and pills, so it seemed to work out. I didn't complain about her problems, and she didn't complain about mine. We both had only one mission each day, to drown out reality.

I never really did go home after the night of the bonfire, even though I intended on going home almost every day. I was just too caught up in my using. It turned into a month and a half long binge that spiraled out of control and led me to rock bottom.

By that time in my life, I had become so addicted to alcohol that I woke up sick every day. It wasn't from a hangover either. If I didn't consume any alcohol, I would start throwing up every five to ten minutes. After drinking four or five beers, I would feel a little better. I had reached the point where I needed to consume alcohol just to feel normal.

Every day, I drank twenty to thirty beers, along with whatever drugs I could get my hands on. I considered myself a somewhat functioning addict. One time, Abbie and I had been up for days on meth and then took a couple hits of LSD each. Abbie wasn't used to that, so I had to watch her kids and play with them while she tried to get herself together. It was seriously deranged to think nothing of taking care of a couple of little kids while sleep-deprived and high on meth and LSD.

It didn't faze me because being high was such a normal part of my life. One time, I was high on LSD when I started to get hungry, which usually didn't happen to me on that drug. I poured myself some Rice Krispies, and as I was eating them, I noticed all of the Krispies moving around. It looked like a bowl full of maggots, but I was so used to hallucinations at that point that it didn't bother me in the least. I devoured the whole bowl and poured myself a second.

Throughout my life, I had also done a lot of inhalants or breathing in chemicals to get high. I had huffed gasoline, Glade air freshener, air duster for computers, and spray paint. When my brother and I were young teenagers, we found something online called the anarchist cookbook. It listed many different recipes for a person to use to get high. One of these recipes was to mix bleach with ammonia. Supposedly, when mixed together, along with a certain type of mold, it would create a gas that a person could breathe in to get high.

My brother and I mixed the chemicals together but never had a chance to inhale anything because it caused a reaction where everything started rising and foaming out the top. It was kind of like you see in the cartoons, where the bread just keeps coming out of the oven overflowing. All we did was make a huge bleach stain on the carpet.

I'M TOTALLY BAFFLED when I think about all the idiotic things I have done to get high. On one occasion, my mom had taken me to Walmart to go shopping because there was no way I could drive. I had been inhaling air duster on and off that day, and it depletes the oxygen in your brain, causing your brain to think you're drowning. With that comes all kinds of ringing and noises that sound like someone is playing a pinball game in your head, as well as a lot of hallucinations.

On this day, I was convinced that someone was trying to steal our car, and I began yelling and cussing across the Walmart parking lot at someone who wasn't even there. The crazy thing is that I was in the car that I thought was being stolen across the street. My mom kept telling me that no one was there, but my mind was playing tricks on me.

That same day, she saw me take a few puffs of the air duster and started to freak out on me. As she was doing so, I fell out in the car. My mom said I went from talking to being completely unresponsive. She drove all the way across town to the hospital because she thought I had died. Right before we reached the hospital, I came to again.

I cannot imagine all the stress and worry I put my mom through. When a person is that engulfed in drugs, there is no rational thinking or remorse, just delusional bondage. The devil holds you wrapped up in chains like a slave.

After my mom had dropped me off that day, I stayed up all night on meth. Then I went to Doug's house to drink and do some more speed. On the second night of no sleep, I drank beer the entire night, and then we all decided to go back to my girlfriend's place and continue the party there. By this time, I had been up for over two days on meth and had been drinking for 24 hours straight.

One of Abbie's favorite pills was Xanax. She ate them like candy. She often fell asleep and became unresponsive, sometimes so unresponsive that it kind of worried me. On this night, I saw her take quite a few of them already and didn't think she needed any more, so I decided to take a walk to get a bag of weed from Spencer for her instead.

I had hidden her pills before leaving, and when I came back, she was furious. She kept asking for them, but I would not hand them over. The longer our argument went on, the more enraged she became. The next thing I knew, she had taken a thick, ceramic dinner plate and shattered it over my forehead.

With all the drinking and drugs in my system, it didn't faze me a bit. I began to feel blood pouring down my face from the massive gash in my head. It was getting everywhere. Abbie followed me around the house, threatening me with a baseball bat, as I began trying to collect my belongings and get out of there. I really thought that she would strike me with it at any minute. Eventually, I just gave up trying to get my things and left before she could do more damage.

As I walked away from Abbie's home, I started popping her Xanax. I don't know how many I took, but it was at least five. With all the blood running down onto my phone, it was very difficult for me to call my mom for help. After several attempts, I finally got ahold of her and asked her to come pick me up on the side of the road.

I only made it about halfway home before being met by police officers. At first, all was calm. They started asking me what had happened, and I explained the situation. I stood there for a little while, and then they started placing me under arrest. That is when I went from being calm and cooperative to flipping out on them. My head had just been split wide open, and I was the one being placed in a cop car. I was in a state of pure hostility.

They took me to the hospital to get my head sewn shut, and I cussed them out the entire time they had me cuffed to the hospital bed. I called them pigs, pieces of trash, and many other not-so-nice things.

After my head was sewn shut, they took me to jail. As we approached the jail, I spit on an officer through the metal wiring because she was accusing me of all kinds of things I hadn't done. They took me to a room that separates the garage of the jail, where a person is brought in and where booking is. The Xanax was starting to catch up with me. I remember cussing at a sergeant through the glass window and him screaming at me to shut up. Then I blacked out.

On January 24, 2011, I woke up to an all too familiar scene. There I lay in a room wrapped in steel and bricks, back in jail. As I laid there, feeling like a train wreck, I started replaying the events that happened the night before. It was still early, and breakfast had not yet come, but I heard the iron door's lock pop. It's a sound that I cannot really describe...a sound you won't hear anywhere else, a sound reminding you that you've lost your freedom.

An officer called my name. She was holding a stack of paperwork in her hand. I was to sign my warrants. As I read them, I sat in complete disbelief at the charges filed against me. They had given me three major felonies: First Degree Domestic Assault, Felonious Restraint, and Armed Criminal Action. Each of these carried lengthy prison sentences.

The Armed Criminal Action charge was actually an unclassified felony, meaning it was not a class A, B, C, or D felony. It was a charge in a class of its own, with a range of punishment from a minimum of three years flat—meaning no parole—all the way up to life in prison. I signed the paperwork and sat down on the floor, concluding that my life was over.

They took me out of the holding cell to be strip-searched and put me in new clothes. I wanted to sign over whatever property I had to my mom, but they told me I needed to keep it there until I was released. I told them to look at my charges. I wasn't going home for many years, if at all.

I can understand how someone might think I was guilty of all these charges based on all the other stories I've described in this book. However, this time I was not, although it is only by the grace of God that I didn't commit what I was being charged with. I had been drinking for over 24 hours straight after having been up for a few days on meth. Amazingly, even after having my head gashed wide open and being threatened repeatedly with a baseball bat, I remained completely calm. The only explanation I have for not utterly flipping out is God. In fact, I'm surprised that I hadn't killed everyone that day, including her dad.

Looking back, I can see that God used this situation to bring me to my knees in prayer, to truly change my heart, and protect me at the same time. I was given a $50,000 cash-only bond and sent to general population. When I first walked through the doors of my unit, I saw my cousin, Pat, sitting at a table. He was on his way back from prison and would be released in a few weeks. It was nice having a family member to talk to.

The first few weeks were absolutely horrible. I had incredibly bad withdrawals from the alcohol. I'm amazed that I didn't need to go to the hospital. My body shook severely for almost two weeks. It was so bad that I could barely get food to my mouth before it would fall off the utensil. I also spent most of my first two weeks just lying in bed, thinking of the horrible situation I was in. It's probably about the worst feeling a person could ever have, wondering if they could possibly spend the rest of their life locked away in a cell.

I was actually innocent for once, but I grew up in church knowing that you will reap what you sow (Galatians 6:7). Even though I was innocent of my most recent charges, I knew that I had done enough in my life to deserve being locked up indefinitely. It's amazing how I knew right from wrong but had drifted so far that I totally disregarded any of my previous morals. There were times when I would stop and consider that I would one day go to hell, but it didn't bother me a bit. The thought would leave my head as quickly as it came in.

Eventually, however, those kinds of thoughts quit happening. I reached a point where I no longer had any thoughts or convictions about what I was doing. It was like God had turned me over to a reprobate mind, just as it says in the book of Romans.

"Even as they did not like to retain God in their knowledge, God gave them over to a reprobate mind, to do those things which are not convenient."

—ROMANS 1:28

After beating myself up mentally for a few weeks, I finally came to a point where I realized the life I had led was not the life I wanted. I knew that I needed God back in my life. All the other times I had been locked up, I never really cared. Of course, I didn't want to be in jail, but I didn't care enough to change. It had just become part of life. Every time I got out of jail, I knew I would be back again someday. It was just a matter of when.

To illustrate just how much jail had become a part of me, one day, when I was hanging out in the unit, I told everyone I was going home to go to bed. They all looked at me and said, "Home?" To me, it was no longer just a jail cell. It was my home. I had become comfortable with it.

This time was different, however. I was as low as I could get. But in this low state, I was finally able to sincerely pray for God's help and guidance. At the time, I felt like I was experiencing the worst thing that could ever happen to me, but I know now that it was the best thing. I wouldn't take that life-changing experience back for anything.

That night, I prayed to God with a sincere heart for the first time. Then I went to bed. The next day was phenomenal. I woke up with a remarkable sense of peace covering me. This was quite a change from the instant anxiety and depression I felt every time I woke up to another day in my jail cell. I felt a peace like I had never known, and I remember going to the rec room and running in circles.

As I ran around the rec room, a radiant joy filled me. I kept thinking, "I wish my accuser could see how happy I am right now." From that point on, everything was different. There were days that I still got down, but I had a hope that, no matter what happened, even if I never got out, things would somehow be okay.

There can be a lot of challenging times while behind bars, but there can also be some decent times if you can make the best of it. I always tried to keep myself in a routine. Most days, I would rise early, do some cleaning, and wait for breakfast to arrive. After eating breakfast, I would try to work out most of the morning and get a shower in just before lunchtime.

For the remainder of the day, I would keep myself occupied with reading, writing, and, most importantly, drawing. It was easy for me to lose track of time while drawing. I enjoyed taking Kool-Aid or the color off of M&M's to paint with. I made a lot of money by selling painted envelopes for other inmates to send home to their significant others.

We had a few board games and also played cards. After lockdown, I would sometimes play Battleship by yelling out the coordinates under the cell door to another inmate next door. I also had some fun giving my cellmate a hard time. He was a gangbanger, originally from Chicago, and had moved to Saint Louis, where he was arrested for selling heroin. He was also a narcoleptic and would fall asleep in the middle of doing anything. I have never seen anything quite like it.

I often would take things out of his hands or move stuff around on him when he fell asleep. He would always wake up confused as to what had happened. Thankfully, he took it well. Sometimes in jail, one must find a way to take their mind off all the depressing thoughts that tend to flood in.

One time, in the early morning hours, something happened that I will always remember. It was as quiet as could be, but from one of the cells, someone yelled out, "Lean on me." Then everything went quiet again until another yelled out, "When you're not strong." And then from another cell, "And I'll be your friend." Before long, the entire unit was passionately singing in unison at the top of our lungs.

It was an unprecedented, remarkable moment. For that brief time, everyone had put aside their differences and joined together to lift one another up. We were all combatting feelings of loneliness, hurt, and failure. Those were the milestones that gave me hope to persevere another day.

I went to several court hearings and asked for a bond reduction every time, but I was always denied. Finally, after over three months, they brought Abbie in to be put on the stand. She got up there and told lie after lie, which she got caught in. There was no way to escape it. The judge was finally starting to see the truth and all the discrepancies in the case.

After hearing her testimony, the judge gave me an immediate bond reduction from $50,000 cash to only $500. After watching Abbie's lying fiasco, I thought all the charges should have been dropped. However, I was still very pleased with knowing that I could get out of jail. I was bonded out the following morning.

Upon being released, I was to report to my probation officer, but my mom and I decided to get some breakfast before going to see her. I was so happy to be free and had no concerns about going to the probation office since I had just been released. But as soon as I had gotten through the doors and turned the corner, I was met by police offers.

My heart sank. Once again, this was an all too familiar scenario for me. I knew something wasn't right. In the little time since I had gotten out, they had issued a probation and parole hold on me, which had no bond at all. It meant I could not get back out. I found myself back in the same cell with the same cellmate before lunchtime. I was completely disheartened. All my hopes had been shattered.

A few days later, I had a meeting with my probation officer about what was going on. She told me the prosecuting attorney did not want to let me out. I was pretty upset about the whole situation, especially since she knew, after hearing Abbie testify, that I didn't do what I was accused of. On top of her preposterous testimony, she didn't have a single mark on her. I was the only one with any injuries, yet I was the one sitting in jail.

With much negotiating and just a glimmer of hope, my attorney tried his best to get me released. I was eventually given another bond for $500, with the stipulation that I would have an ankle bracelet put on and be on house arrest until the case was settled. It was a hard deal to get worked out because my probation had been revoked. Without probation, I would have to pay $30 a day for the bracelet, which I could not afford. But the Lord worked it out, and I was reinstated back onto my probation, so the bracelet cost would be covered by the state.

I was released once again and required to report to my probation officer. It was late when I got out, so I was to go first thing in the morning. I felt very anxious that night, as if something was going to go wrong and I would be back in jail by the next morning. Thankfully, when I went to see my probation officer this time, I was not greeted by police officers. They attached the big box to my ankle, and I was free to go home at last.

Visitation at Jefferson City Correctional Center
(Maximum Security)
Jefferson City, Missouri
November 26th, 2010

"PRAISE YOUR WAY OUT"

Trials will come
And trials will go
But they will end
And melt like snow

Some are just life
And some from above
Whichever they may be
You must not forget the Lord's love

He is there waiting
To pick you up
He wants you to sit at the table
And drink from His cup

Life's full of hurt
And so much pain
But Jesus went before you
He was the innocent Lamb slain

Trials bring you to your knees
To a place of prayer
To pull you out of the pit
Of the devil's fiery lair

He made a way for us
A way to break out
Of these heavy chains
With a praise and a shout

This is the way
The battles are won
Stick a fork in it devil
You are done

So lift up your voice
Raise your hands in the air
You are no longer prey
To the wicked one's snare

CHAPTER THIRTEEN

A NEW SONG

When I was first put on house arrest, I was on a tight leash. I was not allowed many hours out a day. All I really cared about was being able to go to church. It had been twelve years since I had gone. Thankfully, I was given permission to go to church once on Sunday and on Wednesday. However, I was only allotted a certain amount of time, so I needed to come directly home after church was finished. It felt so good to be around a group of people that loved God. Everyone at the church welcomed me with open arms and made me feel loved and comfortable.

The church I was going to offered classes for all sorts of things, which I did not know at first. Not long after being out, my probation officer called me and said that I needed to enroll in some classes for anger management and substance abuse. She gave me the name and number of who I was to call.

I was dumbfounded when I heard the name. It was an old Sunday school teacher that I used to harass and cause problems with right before I walked away from the church. I thought to myself, "Oh great, he isn't going to be happy to hear from me," but I reluctantly gave him a call. I told him who I was and explained my situation. To my astonishment, he was actually very enthused to hear from me and excited to be able to help.

Everything seemed to be orchestrated by God. I would be going to classes with people I knew from my childhood, and the classes would be held at the same church I was already attending. It couldn't have worked out more perfectly.

"In all thy ways acknowledge him, and he shall direct thy paths."

—PROVERBS 3:6

I started going to the classes every Friday night and really enjoyed them. Not only did I enjoy the teaching, but the fellowship was great as well. Each night, they would have all sorts of food set out for the students. Many people from the church were there, too, who just wanted to reach out and love hurting people. Friday nights at the church provided an inviting environment that I looked forward to each week.

Before I was ever released from jail, I decided to get rid of all my tattoo equipment and never get another one. I felt conviction from the Lord after reading Leviticus 19:28, where it says, *"Ye shall not make any cuttings in your flesh for the dead, nor print any marks on you: I am the LORD."* I believed the words of Hebrews 13:8, *"Jesus Christ is the same yesterday, and to day, and for ever,"* and I knew that He didn't want me to continue getting tattoos.

One of my teachers started talking to me about being baptized. I had been baptized as a very young child, but I wanted to be baptized again. It is an act of faith, and I barely remember having it done as a kid, nor did I fully understand what I was doing. As the Bible says, I needed to know and believe what it meant.

"He that believeth and is baptized shall be saved; but he that believeth not shall be damned."

—MARK 16:16

I can be baptized, but if I did not believe and do it as an act of faith, it was no good.

I was never a person who liked a lot of attention, usually preferring to sit on the back row and stay out of view of everyone else. This made it hard for me to get up in front of everyone to be baptized. Whenever there was an altar call at the end of a church service, I would feel God tugging on my heart, prompting me to walk to the front of the church and surrender myself to His will. But I kept resisting this pull of God on my heart because it was so outside of my comfort zone. I was a person who ran from authority, and I didn't know how to surrender my will.

This went on for a month or more. I would stay in my seat during the altar call and then leave church feeling sick. I knew what I was supposed to do. I knew what I wanted to do, but I was afraid.

After weeks of feeling completely depressed about turning away from God, I decided I was done running. I was going to surrender my life to God. No more saying it and backing out. The next Sunday service, I was going to be rebaptized.

The following Sunday was June 12, 2011. It was Pentecost Sunday. Pentecost comes from the Greek word Pentekoste, meaning fiftieth. Pentecost refers to the fiftieth day after Passover for the Jewish people. It was also the day that God poured out His Spirit on people for the first time.

"And when the day of Pentecost was fully come, they were all with one accord in one place. And suddenly there came a sound from heaven as of a rushing mighty wind, and it filled all the house where they were sitting. And there appeared unto them cloven tongues like as of fire, and it sat upon each of them. And they were all filled with the Holy Ghost, and began to speak with other tongues, as the Spirit gave them the utterance."

—ACTS 2:1-4

When Pentecost Sunday came around, I was nervous and excited all at the same time. I would be getting baptized and just knew I would receive the Holy Ghost. Because I wouldn't need my cigarettes anymore, I threw them in the trash and got cleaned up for church. I was on my way to a new life.

The church service was powerful, and I was to be baptized about halfway through. The fact that I was wearing an ankle bracelet made me a bit nervous because they were not to be submerged underwater. If it got destroyed, I could get violated. But despite the worries, I knew I had to do it. I couldn't keep waiting, so I trusted God to protect the device as I was obedient to His will.

I was baptized in the name of Jesus, which is the only way the apostles baptized anyone in the entire Bible. In fact, when Paul had learned that some disciples had been baptized according to another baptism and not in the name of Jesus, he actually had them rebaptized.

"And he said unto them, Unto what then were ye baptized? And they said, Unto John's baptism. Then said Paul, John verily baptized with the baptism of repentance, saying unto the people, that they should believe on him which should come after him, that is, on Christ Jesus. When they heard this, they were baptized in the name of the Lord Jesus."

—ACTS 19:3-5

Speaking about the name of Jesus, Peter stated in Acts 4:12, *"Neither is there salvation in any other: for there is none other name under heaven given among men, whereby we must be saved."* People pray in the name of Jesus, preach in the name of Jesus, and worship in the name of Jesus. Why wouldn't they be baptized in the name of Jesus?

"And whatsoever ye do in word or deed, do all in the name of the Lord Jesus, giving thanks to God and the Father by him."

—COLOSSIANS 3:17

Jesus is the only saving name.

As the service was ending, the music began to play. I could feel God pulling at me again. This time I nervously made my way to the front of the church, closed my eyes, and lifted my hands in surrender as I began to pray. Tears began to well up and roll down my face. I felt God's presence so strongly, but I did not receive the Holy Ghost that morning. However, I planned to go to a big church rally that evening at The Sanctuary Church in Saint Louis, and I just knew that I would receive the Holy Ghost that night. I spent the whole afternoon reading my bible and praying.

The evening arrived, and I went to the service. The Spirit of the Lord was moving. I loved the feeling of being surrounded by godly people who were all worshiping the Lord. As the preaching drew to a close, I was very eager to get to the altar. What I once was afraid to do had become what I desired the most.

Many people who were seeking the Holy Ghost, myself included, had gathered around the front of the altar. I was already lifting my arms and praying as the preacher was still speaking. He said that he was going to pray a prayer of faith, and when he was finished, the Spirit of God would fall on everyone.

My faith did not waver that evening. I believed every word he said, and when he had finished speaking, the Holy Ghost did fall on me. I began to speak in other tongues, just as the Bible says will happen to those who believe.

"And these signs shall follow them that believe; In my name shall they cast out devils; they shall speak with new tongues."

—MARK 16:17

God chose speaking in tongues as a sign of being born of the Spirit. John 3:8 states, *"The wind bloweth where it listeth, and thou hearest the sound thereof, but canst not tell whence it cometh, and whither it goeth: so is every one that is born of the Spirit."* Just like you cannot see the wind, but you can hear it and see its effects, so it is with the infilling of the Holy Ghost. You cannot see the Spirit of God, but you can hear the sign…speaking in other tongues. It is not something that is learned or made up. It is not something that was only for the people in the book of Acts to experience, but it is still very real and happening today. I've experienced it, and the Bible says it is a promise to everyone.

If you are reading this and have never had this experience, I pray that you will ask God to fill you with His Spirit. Peter preached about this experience in Acts 2:38. Then he went on to say in Acts 2:39, *"For the promise is unto you, and to your children, and to all that are afar off, even as many as the Lord our God shall call."*

That night, I left glowing and full of joy. I had been listening to some of my mom's old tapes by Lance Appleton days before, and that night, I had the song "Heart Set on Heaven" stuck in my mind. As I was trying to go to sleep, I could not stop singing it in my head. This went on for hours. I was just so filled with joy that I could not contain it. I remember saying, "God, this is really cool, but I'd like to go to bed now."

The next morning, I woke up in the same state of mind. I had a bracelet on my ankle, and I was facing possible life in prison, but I was just as happy as could be. The house arrest caused me to be stuck inside most of the time, but I didn't let that bother me anymore. I would listen to my Christian music and find a project to do. I found something that my soul had desired all my life, the Spirit of God living inside me.

Me seeking the Holy Ghost Sunday morning.
Cornerstone Apostolic Church | Wentzville, Missouri
June 12, 2011 | Pentecost Sunday

Where I actually got the Holy Ghost on Sunday night.
The Sanctuary | Hazelwood, Missouri
June 12, 2011 | Pentecost Sunday

"JEHOVAH-RAPHA"

Purge with hyssop
The old dope fiend
Remove the leaven
And make thou clean

Let me hear joy
It's been so long
Wake me up
To sing a new song

Make me to have rule
Over my heart
Protect it like a fortress
That cannot be torn apart

Direct my paths
Shine your light on me
Lead me to your door
And give me the key

Wash away my sins
Mold a new man
Give me the strength
To fulfill your perfect plan

Restore my soul
And the years I lost
Keep me from the pit
Whatever the cost

Thank you, Jesus,
For stretching out your hand
And for leading me to
The Promise Land

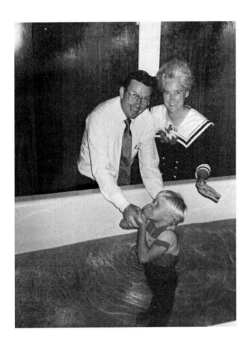

*Me being
baptized as a kid.
Brother and
Sister Willis
Lockport Illinois*

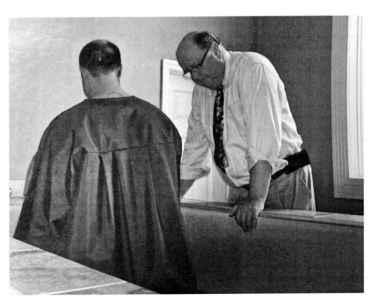

*Me being rebaptized by my then Pastor, Loy McCarty
Cornerstone Apostolic Church | Wentzville, Missouri
June 12, 2011 | Pentecost Sunday*

CHAPTER FOURTEEN

JEHOVAH-JIREH

As the weeks and months continued, I grew closer and closer to God. All I wanted to do was be at church or read the Bible. I would literally read and study the Bible for five to six hours a day.

There were many times Spencer would call me up to see if I wanted to hang out. At times, I was tempted to because of all the time I spent in the house by myself. He was the friend that had taken the possession of marijuana and digital scale charge for me, so saying no made me feel really bad. He had taken a bullet for me, and I was pushing him away. I felt like I wasn't being a loyal friend.

On the other hand, I also knew that I needed to stay focused on God and that going back to my old ways could cause me to lose everything. After telling him that I needed to just stay to myself, I was surprised to see that he understood. Very few people from that kind of lifestyle would ever understand and care enough to respect my wishes.

I had gotten to the point of seeking God so often that all I had to do was lift my hands, and His spirit would instantaneously fall on me. I didn't have to pray for it or anything. I would just lift my hands, and there it was.

Things in my life were going very well. I was completely motivated to move forward and let God transform my life for the better. Though I was still on house arrest, I was gradually granted more hours out of my house until I could stay out the entire day. God had given me much favor. It felt almost as though I wasn't even on house arrest.

After everything that had happened with my last girlfriend, having a relationship was the farthest thing from my mind at the time. However, a woman at my church made it known to someone else that she was interested in me. One thing led to another, and in a short amount of time, I was back in a relationship.

At first, it seemed like a good thing to have companionship. Now that I look back on it, I realize I should have continued to just focus on God.

"But seek ye first the Kingdom of God, and His righteousness; and all these things shall be added unto you."

—MATTHEW 6:33

When you put God first, everything else falls into place.

Her name was Madelyn. She smoked cigarettes, which I had given up. I still had no desire to smoke, but after a while of being subjected to it, all it took was for us to get into an argument. In a vulnerable moment, I made the very poor choice to smoke a cigarette. After I did, feelings of guilt, shame, and failure entered my mind. I didn't fall back into smoking right away, but over time, I gave in more and more until I was hooked again.

Every week, I would go to church and tell myself that I was done with smoking, but I went back to it every time. It was a horrible curse that would follow me for years to come. I still went to church any chance I could get, but the closeness I once had with God was stretching thinner and thinner. I could no longer get in tune with Him with the same ease or hear His voice as I used to. We cannot be full of God when we fill ourselves with sin and tarnish God's temple.

It was around this time that God began speaking to me through dreams. The bible talks about this happening.

"And it shall come to pass afterward, that I will pour out my Spirit upon all flesh; and your sons and your daughters shall prophesy, your old men shall dream dreams, your young men shall see visions."

—JOEL 2:28

The dreams God used to speak to me started out relatively simple, but they became more and more intricate over time.

Madelyn and I were both struggling with smoking, and one night, we decided to pray together about overcoming the addiction. That night, I had a dream, and in it, hornets were flying out of a hole in the ground. They aggressively bombarded my head, stinging me. I kept trying to swat them away, but they just kept coming. I was unable to stop them. Then I saw a hand place a bible over the top of the hole, and the hornets could no longer get to me.

When I woke up, the dream was embedded in my mind. It felt different than any other dream I had ever had. Something in my spirit told me it was divinely given to me. Then God spoke and said that I needed to get back into His word, and it would protect me from the enemy's attacks. Many battles in life are spiritual, and they need to be fought in the spirit. 2 Corinthians 10:3-4 says, *"For though we walk in the flesh, we do not war after the flesh: For the weapons of our warfare are not carnal, but mighty through God to the pulling down of strongholds."*

The relationship with my girlfriend moved quickly and was motivated by our emotions. We were already wanting to get married after only six months of dating. Many people suggested that we wait, including my pastor. Sadly, we did not listen to counsel. We were married in April of 2012, almost a year since I had gotten out of jail.

Proverbs 11:14 says, *"Where no counsel is, the people fall: but in the multitude of counsellors there is safety."* If your pastor gives you counsel not to get married or to take it slower and pray more about it, then you should listen. He was given to you by God to watch over your soul, and there is safety in the multitude of counsellors. The person you marry will affect the rest of your life and could affect the destiny of your soul.

A few months before getting married, I had another one of my court hearings. The prosecutor stood before the judge and told him that she knew she was not supposed to do this, but she would anyway. She then filed a new felony charge on me of Unlawful Use of a Weapon, and she had even gotten a grand jury indictment on me to back it up. I couldn't believe it. As if they hadn't done enough to me already.

The only positive thing that happened that day was I was able to get off house arrest. The box I had wrapped around my ankle for ten months was finally removed. That meant I could come and go without watching the clock to make sure I didn't step outside before it was time. Receiving the new charge was a difficult blow, but I tried my best to keep a positive attitude about it.

Madelyn and I had only been married for a short time when we found ourselves constantly getting into arguments. Many times, Madelyn would just completely disappear for days or weeks, and I would have no idea where she was. I was still dealing with the court, and she was just one more thing I had to stress out about. My choices were starting to diminish the joy and peace I once had.

Over the past year, the prosecutor had not made any offers about what she wanted to happen to me. I honestly didn't care either. I knew what I was charged with was completely absurd, and I had every intention of going to trial. I was not going to just sign my life away this time.

Shortly after the new charge, I was given a new probation officer. I didn't know it at the time, but my new probation officer had been roommates with the prosecutor in college. After several months of seeing her, she began to believe that I wasn't guilty. Not only that, but she saw I had a true desire to be a better person. She then began speaking to her old roommate in my favor. It just goes to show that, even when you can't see it, God is still working. Don't lose hope in the middle of your storm just because you can't see the end result. Have faith that God is on the move.

Before long, I received a call from my attorney, who was actually a public defender, because I didn't have the money to hire my own. He told me that the prosecutor had made an offer. She was offering 120 days in prison and five years of probation. She went from wanting to give me life in prison to only four months if I pled guilty to one charge. It showed me that she knew the charges she had on me were ridiculous. Still, all she cared about was getting another conviction to place on her resume, regardless of what it meant for true justice. It felt like a slap in the face. Even so, it was a move in the right direction.

I told my attorney to tell her that there was no way I would take the plea deal. I didn't think I should have to take any kind of deal because I was not guilty. But I also said to tell her that the only way I would agree to a deal is if jail or prison time were off the table. I would not spend another day of my life in a cell again unless it was because I lost in a trial.

A few hours later, my attorney called me back. The offer was now five years of probation if I were to plead guilty to the assault charge. She would then drop the other three charges. I was so aggravated that I would have to plead guilty to anything. On the other hand, taking probation instead of risking a loss in trial seemed like a safe bet, especially when the potential sentence could mean life in prison. I just wanted to be free and move forward with my life. In August 2012, I went to court for the last time and was sentenced to five years of probation, but I only did half that due to good behavior.

Though I had done a few little side jobs for a guy at a neighboring church, I had not been successful in landing a good job yet. I was praying for a job where I could avoid being around a bunch of cussing and addicts. Shortly after praying, I received a phone call from a roofing contractor who was a Christian. Apparently, the guy I had done some side work for mentioned my name to him at an out-of-state church conference.

The contractor's name was Evan. He said he had prayed about it, and he wanted to offer me a job. It was a job where I would be surrounded by other Christians. I was so excited, and I gladly accepted his offer. I still didn't have my license, but his partner happened to live about a half-hour from me. I was on his way, so he picked me up every day for work. Once again, God was showing me favor. I had never done any kind of roofing work before but caught on very quickly. Within just a few months, I had gained their trust and was shingling sections of houses all by myself.

In the meantime, Madelyn and I were still having problems regularly. It seemed to be getting worse and worse. We were in the church Christmas play together as husband and wife when she took off with no word and went missing for a few weeks. I couldn't just abandon my commitment and leave everyone else in the play even more short-handed, so I chose to stick it out. Someone else had to be my wife in the play, however. To me, that was one of the most hurtful moments in our marriage. I had to practice and perform a play with someone posing as my wife, all while my actual wife had abandoned me. I had no idea where she was or when she would be back.

I often found out she was staying at her ex-husband's house until the early morning hours, and many of our arguments stemmed from that. There was a huge snowstorm one day while she was still at work. She called because the roads were getting slick, and she suggested that she stay the night at her ex-husband's house since it was closer to her work. When I told her I didn't really appreciate that, she blew up on me and told me I was a horrible person for not suggesting she stay at her ex-husband's. She took off again, and that was the last time I ever talked to her.

I didn't hear anything of her whereabouts for over a month. I sometimes felt like just taking my ring off and throwing it in the Mississippi River, but I continued to pray and wear it in faith that God would heal our relationship. I did not believe in getting a divorce. Every time I prayed about it, I would be led to scriptures like Ephesians 5:25, *"Husbands, love your wives, even as Christ also loved the church, and gave himself for it."* I figured if I loved her like Christ did, then I would have to forgive her. After a lot of praying, I decided to stick it out regardless of the circumstances, but soon, I would find out that it no longer mattered.

I checked the mail on Friday the 13th, and there was a big envelope from a legal office inside my mailbox. When I opened it up, I found divorce papers. My wife had filed for divorce. Ironically, we had also gotten our marriage license on Friday the 13th. It was a bittersweet feeling. It hurt because I knew that meant the end of everything, and there was no more hope of repairing our relationship. At the same time, I no longer had to wonder where she was or what she was doing.

Everything with the divorce moved fairly quickly. We didn't have any kids together, and she was not fighting for anything. We both agreed that we didn't want anything from one another, so we didn't have to appear in court or anything. I had been remodeling a place for us, but I just forfeited all the time and money I had put into it and let it go.

Amidst all of this, I was able to get my hardship license to drive, which was a huge step for me. Even though I lost my driver's license for five years, the hardship license would allow me to drive under certain stipulations. It required that I maintain a job and have a breathalyzer machine installed in my vehicle.

I moved up very quickly with my roofing job. After roofing for about six months, my boss decided to stop subcontracting work for a guy because he was very unrealistic and verbally abusive. This guy had seen how I worked and offered me the job of being his foreman to run his roofing crew. I had gone from never being on a roof to running the crew in a six-month period.

I liked it at first. However, I also did the estimating, ordered material, hired and fired people, and did paperwork. On top of all that, I was not getting paid for all the extra stuff I was doing, and this man had also become very verbally abusive towards me. I could only take it for so long. I started to daydream about getting revenge on him because of how he was treating me. Realizing the job was not healthy for me, I decided to quit.

I figured I knew enough about roofing that I could start my own business and make some real money. One guy told me that there was no way I could just go out and start my own business after just learning how to shingle, but he didn't know the ambition I had inside of me or the favor of God that was upon my life.

I spent the little money I had on filing all the needed paperwork, and I got a registered agent. While I waited for all of that to get approved, I started working at Subway. The job was barely paying for my gas, and I knew that soon I would be unable to pay my bills. If I could not pay my bills, I would lose my hardship license, never to get it back again. I would be forced to wait until my five years were up.

Just when I was on the verge of losing everything, God blessed me again in the nick of time. A friend had given me a number to call about doing roofing in the Saint Louis Carpenters Union, so I met with a company owner and was hired on the spot. I was learning that I didn't always get what I wanted, but God always gave me what I needed. It didn't always happen right away, but He always came through…right on time.

Because of the job opening in the Carpenters Union, I put my business on hold for a time. With my new employment, I was paid by what I had completed on each job, not by the hour. This worked out great for me because I was a very hard worker. Things were going well, so well that I had no need or desire to go anywhere else for the time being.

*Picture on the roof working in
carpenters union.
Wentzville, Missouri*

"MY PROVIDER"

Jehovah-Jireh
You are my provider
Lion of Judah
You are my fighter

You are my God
You speak to me
And give me dreams
So that I can see

Which path to take
Which road to follow
I no longer feel
So empty and hollow

You gave me guidance
And warning signs
Transformed my thinking
And healed my mind

You set me free
From prison and jail
Paid for my sins
On the cross with nails

Thank you, Lord,
For all you've done
For being my father
And making me your son

CHAPTER FIFTEEN

BOUND AGAIN

A few years passed as I kept myself busy working and going to church. I still struggled with smoking cigarettes over that time. Ever since I picked it back up, I didn't seem to have the strength to resist the temptation whenever I had a bad day. It was a constant battle. I would quit for weeks but then eventually give back in. This became very discouraging to me. I wish I could say that God delivered me completely, but that was not the case.

Because I worked in construction, I was not always in the best environment. Many of the people that worked with me were drinkers or drug users. A few years into my time with the union, I was placed with a partner who was a meth user. I knew what he was doing, but I just minded my own business until a strong temptation overtook me one day. I hadn't felt that way since before being filled with the Holy Ghost. I gave in and smoked some meth on the job site.

I felt so guilty after the fact, and I became very anxious as condemnation set in. The devil started whispering lies into my mind that I was a failure and undeserving of God's forgiveness. But Hebrews says:

"Let us therefore come boldly unto the throne of grace,
that we may obtain mercy, and find grace to help in time
of need."

—HEBREWS 4:16

Don't allow yourself to succumb to the lies of the devil that say you can't ask God for forgiveness when you fail. The throne of grace isn't a place we approach when we have been doing everything perfectly. Scripture says that we can come boldly before this throne and obtain mercy and grace in our time of need.

I began doing meth almost every day. I was still going to church because I knew if I didn't, I might slip farther away, never to make it back again. However, I felt completely empty inside. When I lifted my hands or prayed, I could no longer feel God's presence. The preaching didn't seem to touch my heart like it once had. I was becoming numb, and I couldn't seem to stop using.

Being unable to hear or feel God's presence was not because He couldn't reach out to me or hear me. It was because I lived a continual lifestyle of sin and would not turn from my wicked ways. Isaiah 59:1-2 says, *"Behold, the Lord's hand is not shortened, that it cannot save; neither his ear heavy, that it cannot hear: But your iniquities have separated between you and your God, and your sins have hid His face from you, that he will not hear."* The more I sinned, the more it separated me from God.

We cannot continue in our sins and expect God to answer our prayers.

"If my people, which are called by my name, shall humble themselves, and pray, and seek my face, and turn from their wicked ways; then will I hear from heaven, and will forgive their sin, and will heal their land."
—2 CHRONICLES 7:14

We must turn from our evil doings and change our lives. If we truly seek His face, He will reach out and meet us where we need Him.

My work partner and I developed a very high tolerance for meth, so we began shooting it up. I was doing several shots of meth every day. We would even do shots on top of the roof while we worked, with people all around and inside the homes.

With each passing week, I descended further into the misery of addiction. The days were no longer about trying to get work done but rather about getting high. Things got so out of hand that my coworker began cooking meth on his way to work in the morning, so we could finish it off on top of the roof. We almost got caught shooting up many times. Prolonged meth use causes your brain to start playing tricks on your senses, so we could no longer keep a good lookout.

One night, I was at church early for prayer, asking God to reach down and help me. I needed Him to give me a different job, away from the drugs, and I needed Him to give me the mindset to care. I could feel myself slipping away.

After praying for only a few minutes, my phone began to ring. It was my old boss, Evan, the guy I first started roofing for. He had moved to Kansas, and it had been about three years since I'd last talked to him. He asked me what I had been up to and that he had been praying about his business. It was becoming difficult for him to run his business from another state, and he felt like God had put me on his heart to take it over. I was in disbelief at what I was hearing. God had already begun providing for me before I even started praying for it.

I told him that I would love to take it over and that I was just praying for a new door to open up for me. I quit the Carpenters Union and began working for him again. It wasn't just roofing this time, so he would come up here and there to help me with projects. I was learning a lot of new things.

Sadly, I didn't stay clean for long. I started hanging out with my old work partner again, as well as some of my old friends who also did meth. The drug seemed to surround me everywhere I went. I remember praying at the altar in church, asking for deliverance from this horrible addiction. All the while, my phone was vibrating in my pocket with calls from a dope dealer trying to sell me meth. The devil didn't want me to break free from it, and he was pulling at me in every direction.

I was doing between three and five shots of meth a day, far beyond where I was the last time I quit. In the Gospel of Luke, Jesus talks about what happens when a person gets rid of an evil spirit. After the evil spirit leaves, it wanders around, searching for a resting place. Eventually, it tries to return to the same person it once inhabited. If the evil spirit finds that person has not filled his life with Jesus but has left his spiritual house empty, Luke 11:26 says, *"Then goeth he, and taketh to him seven other spirits more wicked than himself; and they enter in, and dwell there: and the last state of that man is worse than the first."*

The human heart must be filled with something. Though God had emptied my heart of evil and filled me with the Holy Ghost, my choice to turn back to sin was sweeping my heart clean of the good things of God and allowing room for evil to enter once again. I could feel the heaviness of the spirits attached to me, as I was again entangled in the chains of sin's bondage.

I believe that sometimes animals can sense or see the spiritual realm. My friend had a dog, and there were times that he would just start growling at me for seemingly no reason. Sometimes when I was just sitting against a wall, and other times, when I was trying to get down the stairs, he would bark and growl at me viciously, not letting me by. The bizarre thing is he was never looking at me. He was always looking just over my shoulder. There was nothing there, but he was seeing something. I believe he saw what I was feeling, the evil spirits that had attached themselves to me.

When all of this was happening, it triggered a memory of a girl I had dated. One time, she called me up in the middle of the night, scared and saying orbs were flying around her room. I had no idea what she meant, and I had never heard of an orb. Her cat was also acting weird, jumping around and swatting at the air. She decided to start recording it with her phone. What she saw on the video recording terrified her. There were little white ball-looking things flying around like little spirits.

They did not show up to the naked eye, but somehow, the technology on her phone picked it up. They would fly around the cat's head and take dives at it. That's when the cat would swat at them. I'd never seen anything like it. But I remembered it when my friend's dog would act this way toward me. I knew there were evil spirits attached to me.

One of my old Sunday school teachers–the one who ran the Life In Focus Program—had moved to North Dakota a year prior, and they had been asking me to come visit them. I decided that I would take them up on their offer. I thought maybe getting away would give me the chance to clean up and the strength to stop using.

The mind of an addict always has a way to justify using, so I came up with a plan. I would party hard, get it all out of my system, and then come back and change. I got a plane ticket and spent the night before I had to leave partying. I only had a few hours of sleep before my alarm went off. I hurried to get ready because I needed to smoke some weed and take a shower, so I would not be detected by the airport security.

I quickly rolled up a huge blunt of weed and smoked while packing my things. Then I took a quick shower, and my mom picked me up for the airport. I ate some hash cookies on the way there. By the time I went through security and arrived at my gate, the cookies had started to kick in, and I was so high I could barely think. I remember one of the flight attendants saying "sir" to me several times before she could get my attention. Thankfully, I made it on the plane with no repercussions and was on my way to North Dakota and to what I hoped to be a clean me.

My time in North Dakota was wonderful. The atmosphere felt different. One morning, I put in my headphones and took a walk to spend some time with God. It was an early spring day. The wind was roaring, but the day still had a comfortable warmth about it. I was hundreds of miles away from all the craziness and worries of my life, and I felt such peace. There was something about being in North Dakota that made me feel like I was in the place I had been searching for all my life.

The church services I attended were great, and I had time to get clean. I felt healthier and had high hopes that things would be different when I returned to Missouri. I just needed to get back, stay away from all my old acquaintances, and be faithful in drawing close to God.

My time there seemed to fly by. It was sad to say goodbye, but I was happy to have a clear head on my shoulders. My plane landed late in the evening, and I was going to stay the night at my friend Rachel's place until morning and then be on my way home. I didn't want to chance being tempted to get high, so I went to bed as soon as I arrived at her place.

Not long after going to bed, Rachel texted me, asking if I wanted to get high. I immediately said that I would pass. Then the idea was planted in my mind, and I could not get it out. Within a half-hour of that text, I had gotten out of bed and stuck a needle full of dope into my arm.

To the person struggling with addiction, stop lying to yourself. You cannot allow yourself to be around the people, places, or things of your past, even for a moment! The devil will jump on any chance he is given to destroy you.

"Neither give place to the devil."

—EPHESIANS 4:27

Do not give him that opportunity!

This time around, things went downhill very quickly for me. I started shooting up massive amounts of meth at a time. The needles were so thick with meth that I could barely get the air bubbles out of them. It was like sludge. I was shooting up about a half gram at a time. If you're unfamiliar with drug terminology, a half gram would be about eight to ten lines worth, depending on how big you made them.

Four or five days passed, and I still had not slept since returning to Saint Louis. I had not gone home either. Sleep-deprived and very delusional, I started getting ready to go to work. It was cold, so I started my truck to warm it up. Then I went down to the basement to do a shot of dope before I left.

The amount of meth I stuck into my arm was enough to keep several people high for days. That much meth should've blurred my vision and caused me to start throwing my guts up. But that's not what happened. Instead, I fell asleep. There was no way I should've fallen asleep after the drugs I had just taken, but I believe God saved me from driving that day.

Later that afternoon, Rachel's granddaughter came home from school and woke me up. She showed me a page of Bible verses she wanted me to have, which was rather odd because she didn't know anything about the Bible. She also told me my truck was still running from that morning. After she left the room, I loaded up another needle and put it in my arm.

This went on for about ten days. The only sleep I got during that time was when I fell asleep that morning while warming my truck up. When I finally made it home, I was out of my mind. I had lost a ton of weight in that short time, and my face was starting to sink in. My body was deteriorating rapidly, unlike it had ever done before.

Sunday rolled around, and it was the third week in a row that I had not gone to church. Before my trip, I kept telling myself, "Next week, I will be at church," but once again, I was getting high instead of going.

As I sat there on my porch, I felt God speak to me so strongly. I heard Him say, "Run. Leave here now." My mind started to race, and I became very anxious. I felt like God said that if I didn't leave, I would be dead or in prison. That was enough for me not to do any more speed that night and go to bed.

For the next couple of days, I smoked pot, trying to cope with the withdrawals from the meth. I had decided I would leave, but not right away. I figured maybe I would go in a month or so. I told my friends in North Dakota about everything, and they said that I could stay with them until I found a place. But I kept making excuses. I would tell myself, "I need to have a job there first," or ask, "How will I be able to take care of myself?"

Because I did not get the point that God wanted me to leave immediately, he had to get my attention drastically. That night is one I will never forget. I was lying in my bed when I heard pounding that sounded like it was coming from the living room. I went to check it out, but when I got to the living room, it was dark and quiet as could be.

This happened a few times, which gave me an eerie feeling. But then I began to hear screaming, and the pounding grew louder. It became so strong that it felt like it was shaking my body. I got up to check the living room again, but there was absolutely nothing going on there. Panic began to rise in me.

I started to pray, hoping it would stop, but the more I prayed, the louder it became. The screaming was absolutely horrifying. It is almost impossible to describe what it sounded like. The screams were full of agony, reminding me of how the Bible describes hell in Matthew 13:42, when it says, *"... there shall be wailing and gnashing of teeth."* It was like hearing hell.

I had heard and seen some crazy things over the years of doing hallucinogenic drugs, but nothing compared to this experience. It scared the daylights out of me. It went on and on, but I was too afraid to look in the living room again. I thought, "If I go out there again, and it's completely quiet, I will lose my mind and bolt out of this house."

The pounding and screaming continued. I thought to myself, "I'm sure going to learn to pray tonight." Since I knew there was no way I would be going to sleep, I grabbed my bible and randomly opened it to the first chapter of Deuteronomy. As I started to read, God began speaking to me again. He talked about all the fears I had about moving, the questions I had about what I would do for money, and the anxiety I had about leaving everything I knew and moving to a place I knew nothing about. He reminded me of how He saved me and brought me out of my old life of bondage the first time and how He fought against the enemy attacking my mind.

"The Lord your God which goeth before you, he shall fight for you, according to all that He did for you in Egypt before your eyes; And in the wilderness, where thou hast seen how that the Lord thy God bare thee, as a man doth bear his son, in all the way that ye went, until ye came into this place. Yet in this thing ye did not believe the Lord your God. Who went in the way before you, to search you out a place to pitch your tents in, in fire by night, to shew you by what way ye should go, and in a cloud by day."

—DEUTERONOMY 1:30-33

God was telling me that He was going to take care of me. He was the God that would go before me and search out a place for me to live. He would guide me, protect me, and fight my battles. He was telling me there was no reason to fear. He was telling me to trust Him.

There are only forty-six verses in the first chapter of Deuteronomy. When I started reading, the pounding and screaming were still happening all around me, and I thought I would never get to sleep that night. I was planning to read the Bible until morning. But it turns out I never made it to the second chapter. God had given me peace and put me to sleep before I finished the remaining thirteen verses in chapter one. I slept through the entire night and woke up the next morning with the lights still on and my bible wrapped up in my arms and held tightly against my chest.

It was one of the most surreal moments of my life. I would parallel it to being in the center of a massive storm and then waking up hours later with the sun shining and no recollection of what happened in between. All I know is there was chaos one moment and peace and calm the next. Jesus had calmed my storm.

> *"And they came to him, saying, Master, master, we perish. Then he arose, and rebuked the wind and the raging of the water: and they ceased, and there was a calm."*

—LUKE 8:24

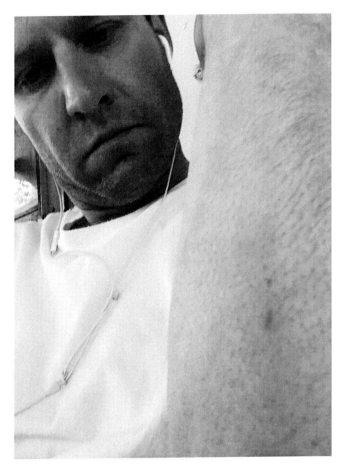

April 14, 2016
After coming back from visiting North Dakota, days
before moving to North Dakota, my face started to
sink in, and my body was deteriorating rapidly. I
was out of my mind on Methamphetamine.

"YOU'RE ALL I NEED"

You go before me
And make a way
Whether it be fire at night
Or cloud by day

You fight my battles
Before my eyes
Answer my prayers
And hear my cries

You led me through the wilderness
And that wicked land
Picked me back up
And gave me strength to stand

You gave me peace
And rest at night
To fall asleep
With your word held tight

You spoke to me
And calmed my fears
In the middle of the war
When I couldn't see clear

I am stronger with you
And my faith has grown much
All I need to do
Is give your garment a touch

I sought you God
And you heard me
You reached out
And now I am free

O taste and see
That the Lord is good
He will rescue you
When no one could

Fret not about
The Evil ones
Cry out to Jesus
And He will come

CHAPTER SIXTEEN

THE EXODUS

That next morning, I woke up with an urgency to leave. The night with the screaming and pounding had been so terrifying that I was rattled by it for the next couple of weeks. I slept every night with the light on, and my Bible laid across my chest.

I knew I had to leave quickly, but I felt horrible about the whole situation. My brother had been in prison for over a decade, and I would be leaving my mom there by herself, which made me feel the worst. I so badly wanted to be there to help her, but it was no longer an option for me.

I called my friends in North Dakota, and they said they would get things ready for me to come. Then I began going through my things, trying to pack only what I would need because I could only leave with whatever belongings I could fit in my truck.

I was also supposed to be signing papers at the bank the following day to take over my boss's business. It was a growing business, and I would have been making a lot of money if I had followed through. Walking away from that opportunity was one of the hardest decisions I have ever had to make, but as I look back on it, I'm positive I would have lost it all with my drug use anyway.

At the time, I was walking away from everything I knew, but I concluded that God would somehow bless me for being obedient. I decided to walk away for the well-being of my soul.

I began tying up loose ends with people, packing up everything I could fit in my truck, and helping my mom with as much as I could around the house before I left. I cried off and on the entire time. I had never known that something I knew was right could hurt so badly. Many times, doing the will of God requires us to lay down our own will because our plans and agendas so often get in the way of what He wants to do in our lives. It took me only three days, and I was ready to go.

On April 25, 2016, early in the morning, I said goodbye to my mom and started my journey to Fargo. I was very depressed. As I drove away into the unknown, I looked in the rearview mirror several times, feeling like I had deserted my mom by leaving her all alone. I kept my foot on the pedal and pressed forward until I was hundreds of miles away with nothing familiar in sight. I didn't know what I would do when I got there, and my mind was racing with questions. But after many miles and hours, I finally arrived where the Lord had promised would be the Land of Milk and Honey for me.

The first few weeks were slow going. My body had been so run down that I slept most of my days away. I would get up in the morning, eat something, and then go back to bed for hours. I was probably only awake for a total of six hours each day. My body needed to repair itself.

When I could stay awake for most of the day, I began searching for roofing jobs. It didn't take me long to find a job on a roofing crew. For a few weeks, everything went well until the owner was arrested for possession of meth. It came as a shock because he didn't strike me as the type. It was also disappointing because I left Missouri to get away from that very thing.

I found myself back at square one with the job search. I thought the time might be right to start my own business in North Dakota. Still, first, I needed to get my entity transferred and have everything approved by the Secretary of State. It was a lot of work. I also had to obtain insurance for my business, which would cost a lot. In the meantime, I started doing side jobs for my pastor and anyone else that needed help, just trying to gather up enough money to get me started.

Things were coming along slowly, but at least they were looking up. Then one morning, before the break-of-day, I was on my way to my pastor's house when a deer ran out in front of me, totaling my truck. This seemed to happen at the worst possible time. I no longer had a way to get to work, and I didn't have the money for a new vehicle or good credit to finance one, for that matter.

The only solution I could think of was to use the little money I had to get a plane ticket to Missouri, where I had an old car sitting there that I could drive back up to North Dakota. I needed money to get the car running again, so I called my old boss from the Carpenters Union. He said I could come back and work for him for a few weeks to raise the money I needed, so I packed what little tools I could fit in my suitcase, and I was on my way back to Missouri. I worked for the Carpenters Union for a week and then picked up a job doing another pastor's roof, which helped me out greatly. I had my car going in no time and was headed back up north.

Before long, everything fell into place for me to legally operate a business in North Dakota, but there were still many challenges ahead. For one, I didn't know anyone and had no contacts for work, so I started by putting an ad in the paper. The other complication was that I only had a little two-door car to pack all my tools in, which I did ever so precisely. I'm sure I looked like a clown show whenever I pulled up to a house to do an estimate. Things were starting out pretty rough, and winter was soon approaching.

I managed to get a few roofs done, which gave me enough money to get an apartment. However, I didn't have the funds to furnish it. When I got my money from the insurance claim for my truck, I used it to get a bed, but other than that, my place was completely empty. I would eat my dinner in bed or sitting on a little metal folding chair.

Despite the struggle to stay afloat financially, I was doing rather well with keeping positive about my circumstances, but one day, I was hurt deeply by some people that I trusted my everything with. I went to church early that evening to pray, but I walked out before the service even started. I was so hurt that I threw everything out the window and began searching for alcohol.

I was back to the same old cycle I had run away from in Missouri. A couple of times, I took off driving all the way back to Saint Louis just to pick up some meth. One of those times, I drove all night to get there after drinking almost an entire twelve-pack of beer. It was a miracle that I made it there safely.

There were many nights I would sit all alone in my empty apartment, feeling like I had no one to talk to. I was hurting and felt I could no longer trust anyone, even though there was a couple at church that I had become very close to. In fact, one of those people became my best friend and still is to this day. But it was a struggle for a while after moving to North Dakota. Even though I knew this was where God had led me, I felt so alone.

I had left everyone and everything that I knew behind. In North Dakota, everything was new to me. I was trying to adapt to my surroundings and not fill my void with drugs like I had always done in the past. It is in these times that we need to learn to lean on the Lord and remind ourselves of all the past trials He has brought us through.

One night, I had picked up a bottle of alcohol and was making mixed drinks while I sat in my apartment feeling sorry for myself. I started writing a poem, as this was one of the ways I would express myself besides drawing. I will include the poem at the end of this chapter. It started off very heart-wrenching, with a sense of no hope because that was how I was feeling, but midway through, I realized how depressing it sounded. I decided that I needed to pick myself back up and end it with victory.

The last time I turned to drugs was the worst experience with drugs I had ever had. I was upset about something, and it just so happened that someone I knew had a bunch of LSD. Instead of leaning on God like I should have, I decided to buy three hits and take them all at once.

Normally, I would have been just fine taking that amount. However, this time was different. About an hour later, as the drug really started to kick in, I started feeling conviction about what I was doing. God had brought me so far, and I was throwing it all away. My conviction turned into extreme anxiety.

All kinds of scenarios started bombarding my head. It felt like a panic attack times ten. My heart was racing, and I felt like I was going to die, but all I could do was try to ride it out. I was starting to have a bad trip, and time seemed like it had stopped. It felt like I would never come down and would be stuck in this calamity.

I went outside to get some fresh air. Everything was moving erratically. There were massive telephone towers across the street, the kind with four sides on them. They looked like giant robots playing tug-o-war with the electric lines as they swayed back and forth. I was going crazy inside my head and needed to talk to someone.

It was very difficult for me to talk, though, because my mind was completely scattered. I managed to call my friends and did my best to tell them I needed them to come see me. I tried to explain how I was feeling, but I was hallucinating very badly. They said they would be on their way as soon as possible.

I started telling God I was sorry and praying for Him to take the effects of the drug away, but despite my pleas, none of it worked. It was about 1:00 in the morning, and I did my best to hold myself together.

As I looked around at the walls, everything was changing sizes as though I was in the middle of a funhouse at a carnival. I tried to read my Bible while I waited, but the words were moving across the pages like water flowing down a river, so I started listening to my Bible app, hoping it would ease my mind.

My friends Barb and Tony arrived after what seemed like an eternity, although it was not more than a half-hour. I was relieved when they got there, but I was not out of the woods yet. As they talked to me, their faces looked like they were melting right before my eyes. They brought a blood pressure machine to check me out, but they said my blood pressure was perfectly normal. All the feelings of my heart pounding and impending death were just my imagination running rampant. They stayed with me for a long time until the effects started to wear off enough for me to think a bit more clearly.

I was FINISHED with drugs after that experience! It would never be the same since I turned back to God. The conviction would destroy every high I was attempting to get. This had been an ongoing attack from the devil, trying to get me to fall back into my old lifestyle. He had been taking shots at me, trying to wear me down and make me give up the fight. In these times of trial, I've learned that we need to be patient, wait on the Lord, and ask Him to renew our strength.

"But they that wait upon the Lord shall renew their strength; they shall mount up with wings as eagles; they shall run, and not be weary; and they shall walk, and not faint."

—ISAIAH 40:31

Shortly after that incident, I dreamt that I was sitting on the church pews, and a demonic creature was walking down the aisle from the front of the church to the back. It was unlike anything I could ever imagine. If you have ever seen the movie "Alien vs. Predator," that's what it was like. It was nasty-looking and massive, standing about nine to ten feet tall. I watched as this demonic being began walking past the pews. Along his way to the back of the sanctuary, I could hear people scream as he started plucking them up out of their seats. It was nothing for him. He did it one-handed with ease.

I was sitting on the opposite side in the back and had ducked down, trying to hide as he made his way towards me. I trembled with fear as he drew closer to me. Boom! Boom! Boom! The ground beneath him rattled with each step. Then he stopped right beside me. I thought he was going to rip me up from between the seats at any moment. But incredibly, he moved past me. Then I heard the horrifying screams of a girl a few rows up as she was snatched from her seat.

I woke up in a panic, heart pounding and sweating profusely. I was no stranger to dreams, but this one shook me, and I was wide awake. Sitting up in bed, I felt impressed by God to open my Bible to the book of Nahum. I had completely forgotten about this book because it's one of those smaller books in the Old Testament that a person doesn't think about too often. However, that is what came to my mind, so I opened my Bible up and began to read. When I got to the end of the first chapter, I was stunned by what I read.

"Behold upon the mountains the feet of him that bringeth good tidings, that publisheth peace! O Ju'dah, keep thy solemn feasts, perform thy vows: for the wicked shall no more pass through thee; he is utterly cut off."
—NAHUM 1:15

It was just like in my dream. The enemy was passing through the church, snatching people up, but when he came to me, he continued on. God was showing me that He had His hand of protection on me. The wicked one did not have the authority to pull me away from the church and into the world anymore. Just like the scripture said, he had been utterly cut off.

To the one who is feeling like a failure, who feels hopeless, who has fallen over and over again, I say shake the dust off and rise again. A baby does not automatically stand by itself on the very first attempt. It falls many times in the trying. We are no different as children of God. Jesus died for our sins, knowing that we would fall.

"Rejoice not against me, O mine enemy: when I fall, I shall arise; when I sit in darkness, the LORD shall be a light unto me."

—MICAH 7:8

That passage does not say "if" I fall, but rather "when" I fall. Failure doesn't have to be fatal. You only lose the battle when you fail to rise again.

"For a just man falleth seven times, and riseth up again."

—PROVERBS 24:16

June 18, 2018
The 2nd year of running my roofing
business in Fargo, North Dakota.

"NOT ALONE"

I sit here lonely
By myself in an unknown land
Seems everything I truly desire
Slips through my fingers
Like grains of sand

I fall down, again and again
Each time rising to my feet

The more I get up
The more I fall
Getting beat down
Not being able to stand tall

Over and over again
My heart is hurt repeatedly
Everything becomes cloudy
And is not easy to see

The Godly voice in my head
Becomes harder to hear
Visions and dreams turn to nightmares
And all I can feel is fear

I can feel the chains
Being wrapped around me
As the devil gives a laugh
And starts twisting the key

All I want to do
Is breakdown and cry
As the years continue to pass
I keep asking, "why God, why?"

Each time I tell myself
Don't listen to his lies
But he knows me very well
Better than a spy

But I have to make it
I have to try
Because in this valley
I cannot die

So once again
I will lace up my shoes
Look up at the mountain
And say, "you won't lose."

This time I will be strong
And I will do more
Till I mount up with wings
And in the sky begin to soar

Because deep down I know
God has a great plan for me
Even though at times
It is hard for me to see

Get up, keep moving,
Don't stand still
The more you press forward
His presence you will feel

You are never alone
In an unknown land
Jesus is always here
Holding your hand.

CHAPTER SEVENTEEN

THE LAND OF MILK
AND HONEY

My first winter in North Dakota rolled around, and it was tough going. I could not do any roofing, so I had to find a different job to get me through the winter. I found a job doing drywall at a college in the next town over in Minnesota. There was no parking there, so I would have to park several blocks away and walk the remaining distance. Each morning, the Northern winter air made it a very long and blistering walk.

Because I was working for an agency that hired anyone to be laborers, I soon started noticing things that reminded me of my past. People on the job site talked about drugs and partying all the time. Though this was not the workplace environment I wanted to be in, I felt like I had no choice but to be there.

I worked there for a few months, but as time went on, I started to despise going to work every day. It was a terrible environment for me to be in, and I was starting to experience temptations of using again. My work situation was no longer viable. I knew myself. If I chose to keep working there, it would only be a matter of time before I fell back into the same old way of living.

I arrived at my parking space one frigid morning, dreading another day at work. As I sat in my car, I struggled back and forth with what to do. I knew the place was not good for me, but I also needed money to pay my bills. I was barely getting by, and I still couldn't even afford to buy furniture for my place.

I got out of my vehicle and started the long walk to work. As I walked, I battled with the thoughts in my head. There was a heaviness weighing on my heart, telling me not to go, and as I approached the building, the heaviness increased. I made up my mind. Though I had no idea what I would do, I decided I couldn't work there anymore, so I went in, told my boss the situation, and walked away. I was worried about my income, but I was relieved to be out of that environment.

Looking back, I should not have had any concerns about my financial stability. There has never been a time that God had not taken care of me, even when I didn't necessarily deserve it. He has always provided for me.

"But my God shall supply all your need according to His riches in glory by Christ Jesus."
—PHILIPPIANS 4:19

God will always provide, especially if you choose not to work somewhere to protect your soul. Never settle for a situation that could jeopardize your spiritual wellbeing. God will honor your decision to choose Him over unhealthy work conditions, and He will bless you abundantly for it.

When I quit, spring was still a few months away. I paid my bills and used what little money I had leftover to place ads for roofing work and prayed that it would all work out. I worked for someone else for about a month to make ends meet, and soon, God answered my prayers. My phone started ringing with roofing jobs.

That first year, I did pretty well for myself. I didn't work every day, but I landed enough jobs to pay my bills and get me through the following winter. I had to pack all my tools into a tiny car and do most of the roofs by myself, but I was happy. God had once again proven faithful to me.

The following year, I was able to get a new truck, and my business doubled from the year before. I could not afford any furniture the entire first year in my apartment. It stayed completely empty, but I was content and blessed. Midway through my second year in North Dakota, however, I was able to move into a three-bedroom apartment and buy all new furniture!

The leap of faith I had taken by quitting my drywall job was beginning to pay off, but greater blessings were yet to come. I just had to keep on pressing a little longer. Many times, we stop just short of our miracles. It wasn't always easy, and my faith was tried on many occasions, but I was learning and growing in the process.

Since branching out on my own, my business has doubled each year, and I've learned that I cannot out give God. Every year I give more, and every year He blesses me more. I am always amazed at how He has provided for me. When I left Missouri, I had to forfeit the opportunity to own a great business that would've made me a lot of money. Still, I just had to believe that God would bless me for turning it down in favor of making the right decision for my soul. I see now, as Ephesians 3:20 says, that He is *"able to do exceeding abundantly above all that we ask or think, according to the power that worketh in us."*

In August 2018, my brother was released from prison after serving a little over thirteen years. He came to North Dakota to stay with me until he could get his feet on the ground. My mom also made the move to North Dakota to stay with me. We were finally all reunited.

He started going to church right away, and on August 26, I baptized him in the name of Jesus Christ, just as Peter preached on the Day of Pentecost. It was done as recorded in Acts.

"Then Peter said unto them, Repent, and be baptized every one of you in the name of Jesus Christ for the remission of sins, and ye shall receive the gift of the Holy Ghost."

—ACTS 2:38

In October, just a few months later, my brother was filled with the gift of the Holy Ghost, just like it happened in Acts.

"And they were all filled with the Holy Ghost, and began to speak with other tongues, as the Spirit gave them utterance."

—ACTS 2:4

In the meantime, I had been praying for direction from God for about a year when I heard about a new church plant being started in the city of Fargo, where I lived. I really wanted to attend and be a part of this new work, but I had not yet received any confirmation from God to do so. Eight months passed, and I still had no word from the Lord.

Then, one Saturday morning, I woke up and felt God tell me the time had come to attend the new church plant. I was so excited. Sometimes it is very hard to be patient and wait on the Lord, but it's much better to wait and make sure you are in God's perfect will.

"Trust in the Lord with all thine heart; and lean not unto thine own understanding."

—PROVERBS 3:5

The little home missions church was just down the road from me. The pastor had moved from another city almost three hours away, and they were having church in his basement. I had never been to a home missions church. There were only a few of us attending at the time, but I really enjoyed it. It was kind of like a little family.

Our services were always touching and spirit-filled. It was a completely different environment than that of a big church. It was more personal but in a good way. We got together for food, games, and fellowship every few months and always had a blast playing a word game that had to do with a lot of guessing. It turns out that almost everyone was quite competitive, leading to nights that were always eventful and exciting.

I was there for about a year and a half when God blessed us with a building to hold service in. There is something special and rewarding about helping a church that started in a home. It is so exciting to see it grow from where it used to be. Before I came, it was just my pastor's family and a couple of other people. Currently, as I'm writing, the church is averaging around thirty people in attendance on Sundays, and it continues to grow.

The first year we were in our building, we put on a Christmas play. It was so cool and so much fun. We had a mix of singing, puppets, and kids acting scenes out. There were many different props, one of which were chains. I had to hold the chains up and break them in the play. The prop went along with part of a song playing, which had to do with being free from slavery and bondage to sin.

Living the kind of lifestyle I lived for so long, sin had been embedded into my mind. Thoughts of my past life and temptations don't always just go away. I struggled with smoking cigarettes for almost a decade. Every time I would quit, days or weeks later, my mind would become engulfed in thoughts of smoking. The thoughts would be so strong that I would give in, almost as though I was a puppet, not even thinking about what I was doing until after the fact.

By the grace of God, I was finally able to shake the temptations, and it had been a long time since I had given in. Then two nights in a row, out of nowhere, my mind was attacked with thoughts of smoking again, and they were very strong. Each time the thoughts came, I would begin to quote scripture and try to block them out. I remember the second night I said, "God, I am resisting. Now I need you to, please, take these desires away from me before I fall again." I withstood the cravings and was able to fall asleep.

Over the years since I've been going back to church, God has given me dreams about different things. He has also given me the interpretation of all my dreams except four. That night, I had two dreams. I don't know how to explain how I know they were God-given and how I know what they mean, but I know they were something spoken to me by the Holy Spirit.

In the first dream, I was shackled to other people with chains. Each of the people represented different types of sin. Then I saw myself in the Christmas play we had just weeks prior. The part I saw was me lifting my hands up and breaking those chains. It was very inspiring to see my own self breaking them. I never imagined that God would use that same scene of me in the play to show me what He was doing in my life. I've had many dreams, but this one was by far the neatest to me.

In the second dream, I was walking around in the grass somewhere. There were snakes all around me, but they were no harm to me. When I woke up, God told me that the first dream represented the chains of addiction being broken off my life. I did not understand what the other dream with the snakes meant, so I prayed for understanding and left it as I headed to church that Sunday morning.

As my pastor started to preach, certain things began to stand out. One of the scriptures he mentioned and put up on the screen was found in the book of Luke.

"Behold, I give you power to tread on serpents and scorpions, and over all the power of the enemy: and nothing shall by any means hurt you."

—LUKE 10:19

Then God began revealing to me the full interpretation of my dreams. They meant that He was breaking the chains of bondage that had held me captive for so long, and He was giving me power and dominion over them so that they would harm me no longer. It was such an amazing moment.

The Bible truly is the Living Word of God, and it is a wonderful feeling when you know God is speaking to you. Since then, I have felt a loosening of the chains in my spirit and have the feeling of liberty.

"Stand fast therefore in the liberty wherewith Christ hath made us free, and be not entangled with the yoke of bondage."

—GALATIANS 5:1

Another dream God gave me had to do with a different struggle I once had in my life. My life was once filled with all sorts of sin, crime, and addiction, and watching pornography was no exception. I had gotten it out of my life, but I awakened to go to the bathroom one night and remembered having a sensual dream. I was mind-boggled as to why I would have such a dream because I no longer have those things in my life. Confused, I went back to bed.

Then I had a second dream. This dream was from God, and it was symbolic, as most of my dreams are. In the dream, I was in my house, and I had a pet black panther. I played with it and petted it. We got along perfectly fine without any attacks, but in the dream, I decided that maybe I should get rid of it before it turned against me one day. So I gently put it outside and shut the door. It began to circle the house curiously as if trying to find another way in. As I watched the panther circle my house, I began going around shutting all the windows and doors, locking them so it couldn't get back in.

When I prayed and asked God to interpret the dream, He told me that the panther represented the spirit I was bound to in the past with pornography. He said that I had let it into my home and entertained it, and now it was trying to find a way back into my life. The enemy doesn't just give up trying to destroy our souls. That's why we must pray every day and put on the full armor of God, so we may be able to withstand these attacks (Ephesians 6:12-18).

One morning, I was awakened a little after midnight and felt a call to start praying. I prayed for about an hour when suddenly, lines of poetry began entering my mind. I was not even thinking about writing poetry, but I knew it was God speaking to me. The lines just continued to come, so I got up quickly and began writing them down. I would realize later that it was the tenth anniversary since I had last been arrested. That day ten years ago altered my life forever.

The poem kind of goes along with my dream about the chains. It also correlates with all the past battles I've fought with the enemy of my soul, how I've been beaten down, broken, and left feeling hopeless. But I know that Jesus fights for me. He will never leave me nor forsake me (Hebrews 13:5). I will leave what God gave me at the end of this chapter.

I am so amazed by the vastness of God's mercy and grace towards me. I feel like God has ordained all of this to come together at this very moment in time. On the ten-year anniversary of my last arrest, God awakened me with the inspiration of a poem. I felt such an immense feeling of thankfulness throughout that day, thinking of how I could have been waking up in a prison cell. Instead, I would be going to church to give God praise.

I could never have imagined being where I am now. As a drug addict with no hope of accomplishing anything in life, I was on a road filled with nothing but pain and emptiness.

> *"Enter ye in at the strait gate: for wide is the gate, and broad is the way, that leadeth to destruction, and many there be which go in there at."*
>
> —MATTHEW 7:13

I had chosen to venture down the path that led to destruction. I had thrown away so many dreams and opportunities and hurt many people with my selfish desires. I had burnt so many bridges and took pleasure in doing so. Anything that didn't suit my agenda was treated with disregard and disdain.

The life events that I've chosen to write about in this book are some of the better ones, believe it or not. There isn't enough room in one book to include all that I've endured and taken part in throughout my life. And so many other things that I simply cannot write about. I should be dead, awaiting my time to be cast into hell for all eternity.

In writing this, I had a difficult time trying to keep everything in the correct timeline. I dug out many folders of police reports, trying to put all the pieces together. Although I did not write about it, there was another time that I went to inpatient rehab. I also went to outpatient rehab six or seven times, but I only successfully completed the program once. And that was only because my counselor gave up and discharged me to get me off his hands.

When I started going back to church in 2011, I went through all my paperwork, so I could stand before the church to testify of what God had done in my life. After doing my research, I found that I had turned myself in almost seventy times to do jail sentences, and those were only the times I physically turned myself in. That did not include the times I had been arrested. Many people believe that you cannot get back all the years in life you wasted, but that is not so with God.

"And I will restore to you the years that the locust hath eaten, the cankerworm, and the caterpillar, and the palmerworm, my great army which I sent among you. And ye shall eat plenty, and be satisfied, and praise the name of the LORD your God, that hath dealt wondrously with you: and my people shall never be ashamed."

—JOEL 2:25-26

I wasted many years and opportunities living a life of sin, but God gave those years back to me. He gave me an abundantly blessed business, and I didn't have to build it for years for the increase. He has also restored my health. When my lungs collapsed during my bad car wreck almost twenty years ago, the doctors said I had the lungs of a seventy-year-old man from all my drug use. Today, I have no breathing issues, and I can run for miles with ease. I have an amazing memory, considering all the drugs and inhalants I used to use on a daily basis. I shouldn't have any brain cells remaining. However, my mind functions as though I've never drank or done a drug in my life.

I have often felt remorse over how I could have helped so many people had I not been living in sin, but God is now opening doors for me to reach others. Because of the lifestyle I lived, I'm able to reach out to those who are drug-addicted or incarcerated. I was recently certified in prison ministries, allowing me to enter jails and prisons to preach the Gospel. I'm also certified to teach anger management and substance abuse classes, the same classes I'd been ordered to attend.

God has taken my life, once horrible and full of sin, and is using it for His glory to reach many people. My past was grim, but my future is bright in God. He took my old, blackened heart, made it clean, and filled it with so much love for other people. I used to be so cold-hearted, not caring at all about others, and now I find myself daydreaming about how I can help others. That is something only God can do.

God can take the worst of people and use them for His glory. Paul, who wrote half of the New Testament, persecuted and killed Christians before his life was miraculously changed by Jesus. He even said that he was the chief of sinners.

> *"This is a faithful saying, and worthy of all acceptation,*
> *that Christ Jesus came into the world to save sinners; of*
> *whom I am chief."*
> —1 TIMOTHY 1:15

If you have walked away from God, I pray this testimony inspires you to return. You are never too far gone that God cannot redeem you. Regardless of how many times you've fallen, you can still get back up. I know what it's like to fail and feel totally hopeless and unworthy of God's grace. Those feelings would tempt me to stay away from the church, but I knew they were not of God. Despite what I was feeling, I continued going to church, knowing things would become much worse for me if I chose to isolate myself from the body of Christ.

The devil wants nothing more than to get you to isolate yourself. He wants to separate you from the protective covering of your church family when you're at your weakest.

> *"Be sober, be vigilant; because your adversary the devil,*
> *as a roaring lion walketh about, seeking whom he may*
> *devour."*
>
> —I PETER 5:8

When lions hunt, they look for the weakest animal in the pack or the one who has strayed away. You are much more vulnerable when you're by yourself. That's why Hebrews 10:25 says, "Not forsaking the assembling of ourselves together, as the manner of some is; but exhorting one another: and so much more, as ye see the day approaching." We need to lean on one another.

The more people standing in our corner during the fight, the better.

> *"Two are better than one; because they have a good re-*
> *ward for their labour. For if they fall, the one will lift up*
> *his fellow: but woe to him that is alone when he falleth;*
> *for he hath not another to help him up. Again, if two lie*
> *together, then they have heat: but how can one be warm*
> *alone? And if one prevail against him, two shall with-*
> *stand him; and a threefold cord is not quickly broken."*
>
> —ECCLESIASTES 4:9-12

If you have never tried Jesus, I encourage you to do so. Jesus is the only one who can truly fill the void in your life. Material things in this world can only provide temporary happiness. They do not fill your heart with everlasting joy. I believe that is why so many famous people, who seem to have everything in life, commit suicide. Despite all their material success, their lives are never truly fulfilled.

I had an employee who lived a life like I once lived. He came to church with me one time, and I tried to get him to do a Bible study with me. I knew as soon as I tried to do that, the devil would put a wedge between us, and only a few days later, I had to fire him due to his lifestyle. I told him that if he continued down the path he was on, he would end up dead or in prison, but he just laughed at me and said, "Oh, is that how you see it? Because I don't see it that way." I said, "Yes, that is how I see it."

This wasn't some kind of prophetic message I had. I just know that jails, institutions, and death are what is promised to a drug and alcohol-filled lifestyle. However, he didn't heed my advice and told me he didn't need my Bible study.

Not long after this conversation, my pastor sent me a news clip with him in it, asking if this was the guy that had come to church. I was stunned. Just 115 days after he laughed at me and rejected a Bible study, he was killed. He was shot while standing outside a bar and died hours later on his forty-first birthday. I didn't realize how badly he needed that Bible study and that God had been reaching for him one last time.

We never know when our time will be up...our Savior today could be our Judge tomorrow. Choose Jesus today. If you have tried everything else in this life, why not give Him a try? I promise, with Jesus, you will have peace in the middle of your storms. Your story does not have to end in sorrow. Allow Jesus to pick up the broken pieces of your life and make something beautiful out of them. All the pain you've endured can be turned into a testimony of hope and transformation that will lead many others to a life in Christ. Do not delay. An abundant life is waiting for you. Come out of the darkness and walk in His marvelous light.

Picture on left:
February 17, 2022
Pensacola, Florida
Prison ministry
conference
Me on left and Bro.
Nicholes Robbins on
right, Head of the
Prison Ministry

Picture below:
April 10, 2022
My first sermon at a
youth service.
Lifepoint Sanctuary
Moorhead, Minesota

"BATTERED BUT NOT BROKEN"

I started my journey
Across the sea
In chains of bondage
Yearning to be free

My ship was battered
Both day and night
No times of rest
Between the fights

I lay on deck
So thirsty from the sun
Alone on the sea
And nowhere to run

I have begun to drift
Straying off course
Being drug away
By an evil force

As the waves crash over
And splash me in the face
I get a taste of the sea
And get back in the race

I break free from the chains
And throw them overboard
I am to be the salt
And was reminded by the Lord

What the enemy meant for evil
Will no longer break me
With Jesus on deck
He can no longer shake me

I have raised my sails
through the waves I go
My ship no longer
Being tossed to and fro

For I will live by faith
And not what I feel
For I know my Jesus
Hath taken the wheel

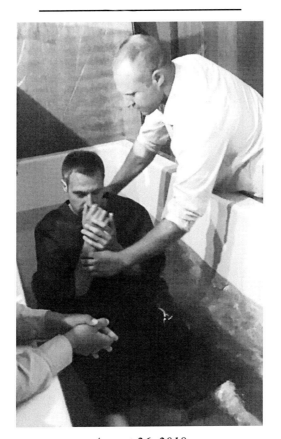

August 26, 2018
Me baptizing my brother after
he got out of prison.
Lifepoint Sanctuary | Moorhead, Minesota

CHAPTER EIGHTEEN

WHAT DOES THE BIBLE SAY ABOUT SALVATION

What will God say when we stand before Him in Judgement? Will He say, *"Well done, thou good and faithful servant: thou hast been faithful over a few things, I will make thee ruler over many things: enter thou into the joy of the Lord,"* (Matthew 25:21)? Or will He say, *"I never knew you: depart from me, ye that work iniquity."* (Matthew 7:23)? Jesus said this also in Matthew.

> *"Not every one that saith unto me, Lord, Lord, shall enter into the kingdom of heaven; but he that doeth the will of the Father which is in heaven."*
>
> —MATTHEW 7:21

WHAT IS THE WILL OF THE FATHER?

> *"The Lord is not slack concerning his promise, as some men count slackness; but is longsuffering to us-ward, not willing that any should perish, but that all should come to repentance."*
>
> —2 PETER 3:9

The will of the Father is that no one should perish and that all would come to repentance. Jesus understood what the will of the Father was at an early age.

In Luke 2, you can read about Jesus, as a twelve-year-old boy, listening to and answering the questions of the doctors in the temple. His parents had been searching for him for three days before they finally found Him at the temple. When Mary tells Him how worried they were about His whereabouts, Jesus simply tells them He had been about His Father's business. What was this business? What did Jesus preach while He walked this earth? He preached:

"Repent: for the kingdom of heaven is at hand."

—MATTHEW 4:17

Jesus came preaching about the Kingdom of God. The miracles He performed and the lessons He taught were about this heavenly kingdom. On one occasion, while He spoke with the pharisee, Nicodemus, Jesus revealed what it takes to enter into the Kingdom of God. This account takes place in John 3.

"Jesus answered and said unto him, Verily, verily, I say unto thee, Except a man be born again, he cannot see the kingdom of God. Nicodemus saith unto him, How can a man be born when he is old? can he enter the second time into his mother's womb, and be born? Jesus answered, Verily, verily, I say unto thee, Except a man be born of water and of the Spirit, he cannot enter into the kingdom of God."

—JOHN 3:3-5

Jesus revealed in this passage that a person must be born again of the water and the Spirit to enter into the Kingdom of God. It has become quite popular to teach that belief in Jesus is all that is required to enter into God's kingdom.

"For God so loved the world, that He gave His only begotten Son, that whosoever believeth in Him should not perish, but have everlasting life."

—JOHN 3:16

This is one of the most frequently quoted scriptures in the Bible. Sadly, it is usually only quoted in isolation, without consideration of the verses that precede it. While believing in the work of Jesus Christ is absolutely essential for our salvation, we must not neglect what Jesus Himself has commanded us to do with our belief. We must be born again of the water and of the Spirit.

WHAT DOES IT MEAN TO BE BORN AGAIN OF THE WATER AND OF THE SPIRIT?

Since Jesus tells us in John 3 that we must be born again of the water and of the Spirit, we need to explore what that means. We see evidence of what Jesus meant by being born again of the water.

> *"He that believeth and is baptized shall be saved; but he that believeth not shall be damned."*
>
> —MARK 16:16

Throughout the book of Acts, there is evidence that the apostles preached and practiced baptism in Jesus' name. To be born again of the water, we must be baptized in the name of Jesus Christ.

> *"Then Peter said unto them, Repent, and **be baptized every one of you in the name of Jesus Christ** for the remission of sins, and ye shall receive the gift of the Holy Ghost."*
>
> —ACTS 2:38

> *"And as they went on their way, they came unto a certain water: and the eunuch said, **See, here is water; what doeth hinder me to be baptized?** And Philip said, If thou believest with all thine heart, thou mayest. And he answered and said, I believe that Jesus Christ is the Son of God. And he commanded the chariot to stand still: and they went down both into the water, both Philip and the eunuch; and **he baptized him.**"*
>
> —ACTS 8:36-38

*"Can any man forbid water, that these should not be
baptized, which have received the Holy Ghost as well as
we? And he commanded them to be baptized in the name
of the Lord. Then prayed they him to tarry certain days."*

—ACTS 10:47-48

*"And he said unto them, Unto what then were ye bap-
tized? And they said unto John's baptism. Then said Paul,
John verily baptized with the baptism of repentance,
saying unto the people, that they should believe on him
which should come after him, that is, on Christ Jesus.
When they heard this, **they were baptized in the name of
the Lord Jesus.**"*

—ACTS 19:3-5

*"And now why tarriest thou? **arise, and be baptized, and
wash away thy sins, calling on the name of the Lord.**"*

—ACTS 22:16

In Acts 2, we see Jesus' disciples first experiencing that new birth
of the Spirit. They were all praying together on the Day of Pentecost when suddenly, they were all filled with the Holy Ghost. The
evidence of their Holy Ghost infilling was that they spoke with other
tongues as the Spirit spoke through them.

*"And when the day of Pentecost was fully come, they
were all with one accord in one place. And suddenly
there came a sound from heaven as of a rushing mighty
wind, and it filled all the house where they were sitting.
And there appeared unto them cloven tongues like as
of fire, and it sat upon each of them. And they were all
filled with the Holy Ghost, and began to speak with other
tongues, as the Spirit gave them utterance."*

—ACTS 2:1-4

The Bible says being born again of the Spirit is what is going to resurrect us when Christ comes back for His church. Romans 8:11 says, "But if the Spirit of him that raised up Jesus from the dead dwell in you, he that raised up Christ from the dead shall also quicken your mortal bodies by his Spirit that dwelleth in you."

We see many accountings of this Holy Ghost infilling throughout the book of Acts. In one of these accounts, we find Paul addressing a group of disciples in Ephesus. They believed in Jesus, but they had not yet received the Holy Ghost. They had not yet been born again as Jesus instructed in John 3.

> *"He said unto them,* **Have ye received the Holy Ghost since ye believed?** *And they said unto him, We have not so much as heard whether there be any Holy Ghost... When Paul had laid his hands upon them,* **the Holy Ghost came on them, and they spake with tongues, and prophesied."***
>
> —ACTS 19:2, 6

There is another account about people being born again of the Spirit in Acts 8. Philip had been preaching Jesus to the Samaritans. They believed His preaching and chose to be born again of the water, baptized in Jesus' name. When the apostles, who were in Jerusalem, heard about the happenings in Samaria, they sent Peter and John to check it out. Since these Samaritan people had already been born again of the water, Peter and John prayed for them that they might be born again of the Spirit. Here is that account in Acts 8.

> *"Now when the apostles which were at Jerusalem heard that Samaria had received the word of God, they sent unto them Peter and John:* **Who, when they were come down, prayed for them, that they might receive the Holy Ghost:** *(For as yet he was fallen upon none of them: only they were*

*baptized in the name of the Lord Jesus.) **Then laid they
their hands on them, and they received the Holy Ghost.***"

—*ACTS 8:14-16*

THE GOSPEL OF JESUS CHRIST

After His resurrection and before ascending into heaven, Jesus
gave His disciples this command.

*"Go ye into all the world, and preach the gospel to every
creature."*

—MARK 16:15

But what does it mean to preach the gospel? Scripture tells us that
the gospel is the completed work of Christ, His death, burial, and
resurrection. The Apostle Paul helps shed some light on this in 1 Corinthians 15.

*"Moreover, brethren, **I declare unto you the gospel** which
I preached unto you, which also ye have received, and
wherein ye stand; **By which also ye are saved**, if ye keep in
memory what I preached unto you, unless ye have believed
in vain. For I delivered unto you first of all that which I
also received, how that **Christ died for our sins** according
to the scriptures; And that **he was buried**, and that **he rose
again the third day** according to the scriptures."*

—1 CORINTHIANS 15:1-4

The Apostle Paul states in this passage that he declared the gospel
to the people at Corinth. In declaring the gospel, he preached that
Jesus died for our sins, that he was buried, and that he rose again. He
also declares that it is this gospel that saves us. We also see him writing about this gospel in the book of 1 Thessalonians. He talks about
the importance of obeying the gospel and the consequences of not
doing so.

*"And to you who are troubled rest with us, when the
Lord Jesus shall be revealed from heaven with his mighty
angels, **in flaming fire taking vengeance on them that
know not God, and that obey not the gospel of our Lord
Jesus Christ**: Who shall be punished with everlasting
destruction from the presence of the Lord, and from the
glory of his power."*

—2 THESSALONIANS 1:7-9

It is clear in scripture that obedience to the gospel is necessary for
our salvation. But what does it mean to obey the gospel? Since the
gospel is the death, burial, and resurrection of Jesus Christ, obedience
to the gospel means we join Christ in His death, burial, and resurrection. Let's explore what that means.

OBEDIENCE TO THE DEATH OF CHRIST

Just as Jesus died (Matthew 27:35-38), we must also die through
our repentance. We must deny our self-will and turn from our sin.
Repentance means to turn away from our old way of life and walk in a
new way. When we repent, we make a conscious choice to quit living
a life of sin.

*"And they that are Christ's have crucified the flesh with
the affections and lusts."*

—GALATIANS 5:24

We must become dead to sin, just as Romans 6:1-2 tells us.

*"What shall we say then? Shall we continue in sin, that
grace may abound? God forbid, How shall we, that are
dead to sin, live any longer therein?" Obedience to the
death of Christ means to repent of our sins."*

—ROMANS 6:1-2

OBEDIENCE TO THE BURIAL OF CHRIST

Just as Jesus was buried after his death (Matthew 27:57-60), we must be buried after our death in repentance. The Bible tells us that this is done through baptism. Romans 6 gives a beautiful description of what baptism means in the life of a believer.

"Know ye not, that so many of us as were baptized into Jesus Christ were baptized into his death? **Therefore we are buried with him by baptism into death:** *that life as Christ was raised up from the dead by the glory of the Father, even so we also should walk in newness of life."*

—ROMANS 6:3-5

OBEDIENCE TO THE RESURRECTION OF CHRIST

Just as Jesus rose again (1 Thessalonians 4:14, 1 Corinthians 15:3-8), we must rise again to new life. The power of the work of Christ was not complete until He rose again. So it is with us. It's not enough to merely die and be buried, but we must rise again to walk in new life. Scripture tells us that to do this, we must be filled with God's Spirit.

"For the law of the Spirit of life in Christ Jesus hath made me free from the law of sin and death... But ye are not in the flesh, but in the Spirit, if so be that the Spirit of God dwell in you. Now if any man have not the Spirit of Christ, he is none of us. And if Christ be in you, the body is dead because of sin; but the Spirit is life because of righteousness. But if the Spirit of him that raised up Jesus from the dead dwell in you, he that raised up Christ from the dead shall also quicken your mortal bodies by his Spirit that dwelleth in you."

—ROMANS 8:2, 9-11

Jesus made a way for our salvation through His death, burial, and resurrection. This is the gospel of Jesus Christ. But as we saw in I Thessalonians 1:7-9, it isn't enough to just know about the gospel of Christ. We must obey His gospel, following him in His death, burial, and resurrection, for the saving work of Christ to have any effect on our lives.

ISN'T JUST BELIEVING ENOUGH?

Many churches preach that our salvation comes from merely confessing and believing that Jesus Christ is Lord. They take this teaching from the book of Romans.

"That if thou shalt confess with thy mouth the Lord Jesus, and shalt believe in thine heart that God hath raised him from the dead, thou shalt be saved."

—ROMANS 10:9

Now, of course, on its own, this verse appears to tell us that salvation is obtained through confession and belief alone, just as many churches commonly teach. The problem with this teaching, however, is it teaches this verse in isolation, not considering where it lies within the greater context of scripture.

In John 5:39, Jesus says to *"search the scriptures; for in them ye think ye have eternal life: and they are they which testify of me."* The reason searching the scriptures—plural—is so important is that scripture sheds light on scripture. If one verse is not totally clear, then we look to the greater body of scripture to deduce the meaning of the verse in question. We should do this even if we think we understand the meaning of a verse because context, or the lack thereof, can alter our understanding of a particular passage. Context matters. That's why it's dangerous to make an entire doctrine about salvation based on one isolated passage of scripture.

My intention is not to degrade anybody's experiences or beliefs up to this point. I hope to encourage people to study and understand scripture for themselves. We must be aware when we're confronted with false teachings, especially when it comes to the topic of salvation. Is there anything more important than the salvation of our souls? Many people preach and teach things that do not line up with scripture. Paul warned the church in Galatia about this very thing.

"I marvel that ye are so soon removed from him that called you into the grace of Christ unto another gospel; Which is not another; but there be some that trouble you, and would pervert the gospel of Christ. But though we, or an angel from heaven, preach any other gospel unto you than that which we have preached unto you, let him be accursed."

—GALATIANS 1:6-8

Apparently, even in the earliest days of the Church, there were people who tried to pervert the true teaching of the gospel of Christ. Paul didn't mince any words about what should happen to those who do this. In the prior section, we covered what the Bible says about the gospel of Christ. It is only through obedience to the gospel of Christ that saves us. The teaching that one must merely believe and "accept" Jesus to be saved ignores the full scope of scripture on the matter of salvation.

Of course, belief is an integral part of the salvation process because one cannot obey the gospel without first believing in it. But let's take a closer look at what scripture says about those who believe yet have not yet obeyed the full gospel of Christ. In Acts 19, Paul comes across a group of people in this very situation.

"And it came to pass, that, while Apollos was at Corinth, Paul having passed through the upper coasts came to Ephesus: and finding certain disciples, He said unto

*them, **Have ye received the Holy Ghost since ye believed?** And they said unto him, we have not so much as
heard whether there be any Holy Ghost."*

—ACTS 19:1-2

Here we find a group of people who believe that Jesus Christ is
Lord, but they have not yet received the Holy Ghost. Because Paul
understood that receiving the Holy Ghost was part of obeying the
gospel, he wanted to ensure that these believers didn't just stop at
believing. When he realized they hadn't yet received the Holy Ghost,
he asked them another important question, "Unto what then were ye
baptized?" (Acts 19:3) Notice that Paul does not ask these believers
whether they'd accepted Jesus as their Savior or prayed the sinner's
prayer. He asked them if they'd been filled with the Holy Ghost and
how they had been baptized. Paul wanted to know if they had been
born again of the water and of the Spirit as Jesus instructed in John
3:5.

Our belief in the saving work of Christ will propel us to do something with that belief. It must be more than a simple intellectual exer-
cise. Faith in Christ will lead us to obedience to Christ. Acts 8 gives us
a wonderful example of how a group of people believed the preaching
of the gospel, and this belief propelled them to obey what was being
preached. They were baptized in the name of Jesus.

*"But **when they believed** Philip preaching the things
concerning the kingdom of God, and the name of Jesus
Christ, **they were baptized**, both men and women."*

—ACTS 8:12

Countless people believe in God. They believe Jesus is the Savior
of the world. They believe He died for the sins of mankind, but how
many allow their belief in Jesus to propel them to obey the teachings
in His Word? A belief that produces no action is insufficient for our
salvation. James writes about this in the second chapter of his epistle.

"What doth it profit, my brethren, though a man say he hath faith, and have not works? can faith save him? If a brother or sister be naked, and destitute of daily food, And one of you say unto them, Depart in peace, be ye warmed and filled; notwithstanding ye give them not those things which are needful to the body; what doth it profit? **Even so faith, if it hath not works, is dead being alone.** Yea, a man may say, Thou hast faith, and I have works: shew me thy faith without thy works, and I will shew thee my faith by my works. **Thou believest that there is one God; thou doest well: the devils also believe, and tremble.** But wilt thou know, O vain man, that **faith without works is dead?"**

—JAMES 2:14-20

James tells us that even the devils believe in God. If merely believing in God is enough, then even the devils should be saved from eternal judgment, regardless of their continual rebellion against God. James goes on to say:

*"Was not Abraham our father justified by works, when he had offered Isaac his son upon the altar? Seest thou how faith wrought with his works, and **by works was faith made perfect?"***

—JAMES 2:20-21

Abraham had faith in God, but it was only after his faith was accompanied by his obedience—works—that God counted him righteous. So it is with us. We must believe in the work of Christ, yes, but the work of Christ will be of no effect in our lives until we merge our faith with obedience to the gospel of Christ.

WHAT DOES THE BIBLE SAY ABOUT BAPTISM?

Is baptism essential for salvation?

It is an often debated subject whether a person needs to be baptized for salvation, but a careful study of Scripture gives a clear answer. In Mark 16, we find Jesus giving His last instructions to His disciples. He addresses the subject of baptism when he says:

"He that believeth and is baptized shall be saved; but he that believeth not shall be damned."

—MARK 16:16

It is clear from this declaration of Jesus that baptism is an essential part of the salvation process.

Jesus also addressed this subject in in the book of John.

"Except a man be born of water and of the Spirit, he cannot enter into the Kingdom of God."

—JOHN 3:5

Here, Jesus talks about two births that are required before entering into the Kingdom of God, one of water and one of the Spirit. Peter addressed both baptisms when he preached on the Day of Pentecost.

"Then Peter said unto them, Repent, and be baptized every one of you in the name of Jesus Christ for the remission of sins, and ye shall receive the gift of the Holy Ghost."

—ACTS 2:38

When Peter preached about baptism, he didn't say it was merely an outward expression of an inward work. He said that baptism is for the remission, or the clearing away, of a person's sins. Without baptism, the record of our sins remains intact. It is only through baptism that our sins can be washed away.

Peter also speaks about baptism in I Peter 3:20-21. He begins by referring to the great flood by which God judged the earth in the days of Noah. Everyone on earth perished in this deluge, except Noah and his family, just eight souls, because they had obediently entered the ark as God had instructed them. Then Peter goes on to say that baptism is just like this. It saves us from the impending judgment that is to come on this earth by cleansing us from our sinful ways.

> *"Which sometime were disobedient, when once the long-suffering of God waited in the days of Noah, while the ark was a preparing, wherein few, that is, eight souls were saved by water.* **The like figure whereunto even baptism doth also now save us** *(not the putting away of the filth of the flesh, but* **the answer of a good conscience toward God**,) *by the resurrection of Jesus Christ."*
>
> —I PETER 3:20-21

As we've seen in the preceding scriptures, baptism is an essential part of the salvation process. Without baptism, there is no remission of sins. Without remission of sins, we cannot be saved from the eternal consequences of our sins.

> *"not by works of righteousness which we have done, but according to his mercy he saved us, by the* **washing of regeneration**, *and renewing of the Holy Ghost."*
>
> —TITUS 3:5

Even Jesus was baptized, though He had no sin, to be our example.

> *"Then cometh Jesus from Galilee to Jordan unto John, to be baptized of him… And Jesus, when he was baptized, went up straightway out of the water: and, lo, the heavens were opened unto him, and he saw the Spirit of God descending like a dove, and lighting upon him."*
>
> —MATTHEW 3:13, 16

SHOULD INFANTS BE BAPTIZED?

Though many today practice infant baptism, a careful study of what the Bible says about baptism leads us to conclude that babies are not yet ready to be baptized. Firstly, we find that baptism is an act of faith. Jesus tells us this in Mark:

*"He that **believeth** and is baptized shall be saved."*

—MARK 16:16

Before a person is baptized, he must first believe in the saving work of Christ. As we know, a baby does not yet have an awareness that Christ died for his sins, so he doesn't have the ability to place his faith in Christ just yet.

Another important aspect of baptism that an infant is unable to partake in is repentance. Peter commands this in Acts 2:30:

*"**Repent**, and be baptized every one of you in the name of Jesus Christ."*

—ACTS 2:30

We must repent of our sinful ways before we enter into baptism, but a baby is not yet conscious of sin, and therefore, he could not possibly repent. Baptism should be an act of faith that follows repentance, so until a child is old enough to be aware of the work of Christ and to understand why that work was necessary, he should not be baptized.

BAPTISM BY IMMERSION VS. SPRINKLING

Another debate about baptism is whether to baptize by full immersion in water or a mere sprinkling of water. Again, we can look to scripture for our answer to this question. But before we delve into what the Bible says about baptism, let us quickly explore what the original Greek can tell us about the process. In the Bible, the word "baptism" comes from the Greek verb, "baptizo," which means to dip, immerse, submerge, or plunge.

As we will see in the biblical accounts of baptism, the first church baptized with the method of full immersion in water, rather than just sprinkling. Accounts in scripture that can shed light on the proper method of baptism speak of people coming up out of the water when they were baptized or choosing a certain body of water for baptism because there was much water there.

> *"And Jesus, when he was baptized, went up straightway out of the water..."*
>
> —MATTHEW 3:16

> *"And John also was baptized in Aenon near to Salim, because there was **much water there**..."*
>
> —JOHN 3:23

> *"And he commanded the chariot to stand still: and they went down both **into the water**... And when they were **come up out of the water**..."*
>
> —ACTS 8:38-39

It is helpful to note that the sprinkling of water in baptism did not become popularized until around 325 A.D. The Roman emperor Constantine I held a meeting with many of the church leaders of that day to formulate and establish an "official" church doctrine. This meeting was called the Council of Nicea, as it took place in ancient Nicea, which is modern-day Turkey.

It was in this council that the idea of the sprinkling of water and baptism in the titles Father, Son, and Holy Ghost were adopted, but these were not the methods of the original apostles in the book of Acts. This is important to understand because God's Word never changes. If we simply search the Scriptures to see what they say about baptism, we will reach a different conclusion than they did at the Council of Nicea.

In Acts 4:17-20, Peter and John are threatened to not speak or teach in the name of Jesus. However, Peter and John said they could not but speak the things which they had seen and heard. Even when being threatened they continued to stick to what they were taught by Jesus.

BAPTISM IN THE NAME OF JESUS VS. FATHER, SON, AND HOLY GHOST

We see that Jesus commanded his disciples in Matthew 28:19 to go and teach all nations, "baptizing them in the name of the Father, and of the Son, and of the Holy Ghost." But when we look at the book of Acts, we find those same men only baptized in the name of Jesus. Though this may appear to be a discrepancy in the Bible, upon closer examination, we find that it is not.

"all scripture is given by inspiration of God, and is profitable for doctrine, for reproof, for correction, and for instruction in righteousness."

—2 TIMOTHY 3:16

Because all scripture is God-inspired and God can never fail, the scriptures He has given us are infallible and without contradiction.

Suppose we ever encounter a passage of the Bible that seems to contradict another part of the Bible. In that case, the fault does not lie with the Bible but rather with our faulty understanding of what we're reading. We must pray for understanding and study the scriptures, *"rightly dividing the word of truth,"* as 2 Timothy 2:15 instructs us to do. Because *"no prophecy of the scripture is of any private interpretation"* (2 Peter 1:20)—meaning we cannot interpret scripture just any way we think best—we must use the whole counsel of scripture to understand the meaning of a particular text.

Let's take a closer look at Matthew 28:19. Jesus commanded his disciples to baptize in the name of the Father, Son, and Holy Ghost. Firstly, the words Father, Son, and Holy Ghost are simply titles and not names. One man may be a father, a son, a husband, an uncle, a brother, or a cousin, but these designations are merely titles that describe the different roles that one man fulfills in his life. Those titles do not tell us his name. Whether he's fulfilling the role of a father, a husband, a son, or even an employee, the fact is that his name remains unchanged. He has many different roles but only one name. Matthew 28:19 tells us to baptize in the name—singular—of the one who fulfills the roles of Father, Son, and Holy Ghost. The question then becomes, what is His name?

John 20:31 tells us *"that Jesus is the Christ, the Son of God."* That means the name of the Son referred to in Matthew 28:19 is Jesus. Then we read the words of Jesus in John 5:43, where He says, *"I am come in my Father's name."* We can infer from this that the name of the Father referred to in Matthew 28:19 is also Jesus. Lastly, if we go to John 14:26, we see Jesus telling His disciples, *"But the Comforter, which is the Holy Ghost, whom the Father will send in my name, he shall teach you all things."* Jesus is telling us here that the Holy Ghost will be sent in His name. What's that name? Jesus. By carefully examining the scriptures, we find that the singular name of the Father, Son, and Holy Ghost referred to in Matthew 28:19 is the name of Jesus.

Acts 4:12 tells us that the only name given for salvation is the name of Jesus.

"Neither is there salvation in any other: for there is none other name under heaven given among men, whereby we must be saved."

—ACTS 4:12

Colossians 3:17 tells us we are to do all things in the name of Jesus.

*"And whatsoever ye do in word or deed, do all in the name
of the Lord Jesus."*

—COLOSSIANS 3:17

John 20:31 tells us we have life through the name of Jesus.

*"But these are written, that ye might believe that Jesus is the
Christ, the Son of God: and that believing ye might have life
through his name."*

—JOHN 20:31

**Acts 10:43 tells us we receive remission of sins through the name
of Jesus.**

*"To him give all the prophets witness, that through his name
whosoever believeth in him shall receive remission of sins."*

—ACTS 10:43

**1 John 2:12 tells us we are forgiven for the sake of the name of
Jesus.**

*"I write unto you, little children, because your sins are for-
given you for his name's sake."*

—1 JOHN 2:12

**Acts 2:38 tells us we are to be baptized for the remission of
sins in the name of Jesus.**

*"Then Peter said unto them, Repent, and be baptized every
one of you in the name of Jesus Christ for the remission of
sins, and ye shall receive the gift of the Holy Ghost."*

—ACTS 2:38

It is helpful to note that when Peter preached baptism in Jesus' name on the Day of Pentecost, he was surrounded by the eleven

other disciples (Acts 2:14) who had also heard the command of Jesus in Matthew 28:19. If he was preaching in disobedience to that command, eleven other disciples who were listening would have corrected him, but they did not.

Another helpful way to view Matthew 28:19 is through the lens of a first-century Jew. As the apostles were Jews, they only believed in one God. The very foundation of their belief system can be found in the words of Deuteronomy 6:4, "Hear, O Israel: The LORD our God is one LORD." The concept of a trinity was foreign to their way of belief. At that time, only pagans believed in a trinity of gods. The Jews' monotheistic religion stood in stark contrast to the pagan religions around them. When Jesus commanded the Jewish disciples that they were to baptize in the name of the Father, Son, and Holy Ghost, they didn't view God as three separate entities, but rather, they understood that He was one God fulfilling different roles. The trinitarian formula of baptism would've been totally foreign to the original apostles, as the doctrine of the trinity and its mode of baptism were not invented until the fourth century A.D.

We can trust that Peter preached the correct mode of baptism because Jesus had given him the keys to the Kingdom of Heaven in Matthew 16:18-19. We find nowhere in the scriptures that follow that God took those keys from him or disapproved of Peter's salvation preaching. God trusted Peter to take the Gospel message to many people in the book of Acts, including a man in Acts 10 named Cornelius, who was a God-fearing gentile. Just as he preached in Acts 2, Peter commanded Cornelius to be baptized in the name of the Lord.

Scriptures on Baptism

"I indeed baptize you with water unto repentance, but he that cometh after me is mightier than I, whose shoes I am not worthy to bear: he shall baptize you with the Holy Ghost, and with fire... Then cometh Jesus from Galilee to Jordan

unto John, to be baptized of him... And Jesus, when he was
baptized, went up straightway out of the water: and, lo, the
heavens were opened unto him, and he saw the Spirit of God
descending like a dove, and lighting upon him."

—MATTHEW 3:11, 13, 16

"Go ye therefore, and teach all nations, baptizing them in the
name of the Father, and of the Son, and of the Holy Ghost:"

—MATTHEW 28:19

"John did baptize in the wilderness, and preach the baptism
of repentance for the remission of sins. And there went out
unto him all the land of Judaea, and they of Jerusalem, and
were all baptized of him in the river Jordan, confessing their
sins."

—MARK 1:4-5

"I indeed have baptized you with water: but he shall baptize
you with the Holy Ghost. And it came to pass in those days,
that Jesus came from Nazareth of Galilee, and was baptized
of John in Jordan."

—MARK 1:8-9

"He that believeth and is baptized shall be saved; but he that
believeth not shall be damned."

—MARK 16:16

"John answered, saying unto them all, I indeed baptize you
with water; but one mightier than I cometh, the latchet of
whose shoes I am not worthy to unloose: he shall baptize you
with the Holy Ghost and with fire... Now when all the people
were baptized, it came to pass, that Jesus also being baptized
, and praying, the heaven was opened."

—LUKE 3:16, 21

"After these things came Jesus and his disciples into the land of Judaea; and there he tarried with them, and baptized."

—JOHN 3:22

"And said unto them, Thus it is written, and thus it behooved Christ to suffer, and to rise from the dead the third day: And that repentance and remission of sins should be preached in his name among all nations, beginning at Jerusalem."

—LUKE 24:46-47

"Then Peter said unto them, Repent, and be baptized every-one of you in the name of Jesus Christ for the remission of sins, and ye shall receive the gift of the Holy Ghost."

—ACTS 2:38

"(For as yet he was fallen upon none of them: only they were baptized in the name of the Lord Jesus.)"

—ACTS 8:16

"And he commanded them to be baptized in the name of the Lord. Then prayed they him to tarry certain days."

—ACTS 10:48

"Then said Paul, John verily baptized with the baptism of repentance, saying unto the people, that they should believe on him which should come after him, that is, on Christ Jesus. When they heard this, they were baptized in the name of the Lord Jesus."

—ACTS 19:4-5

"And now why tarriest thou? Arise, and be baptized, and wash away thy sins, calling on the name of the Lord."

—ACTS 22:16

"Buried with him [Jesus] in baptism, wherein also ye are risen with him through the faith of the operation of God, who hath raised him from the dead."

—COLOSSIANS 2:12

"And whatsoever ye do in word or deed, do all in the name of the Lord Jesus, giving thanks to God and the Father by him."

—COLOSSIANS 3:17

"Know ye not, that so many of us as were baptized into Jesus Christ were baptized into his death?"

—ROMANS 6:3

"And such were some of you: but ye are washed, but ye are sanctified, but ye are justified in the name of the Lord Jesus, and by the Spirit of God."

—1 CORINTHIANS 6:11

"For as many of you as have been baptized into Christ have put on Christ."

—GALATIANS 3:27

"FERVENT PRAYER"

Our Father
Who art in heaven
Give us the grace to forgive
Seventy times seven

Give us this day
Our daily bread
From the moment we rise
Up out of our beds

Let us be filled with mercy
And kindness so true
Help us to fulfill our calling
And be amongst the chosen few

Lead us not into temptation
But deliver us from sin
Keep us from the pit
And let us not fall in

Give us your heart
And give us your eyes
Give us the discernment
To see through all Satan's lies

Help us be the light
In this world so cold
That we may lead others
To your riches untold

Cleanse our lips
Let them speak peace
Let us lift others up
And our prayers never cease

May Your kingdom come
And thy will be done
For the war against evil
Has already been won

For yours is the power
And glory forever
May we be filled with Your Spirit
The earnest of Your treasures

PRAY UNTIL...
